Genealogy

Family Tree Research Made Easy

By Poppy Sure

Copyright and Trademarks

Disclaimer and Legal Notice

Foreword

My personal love affair with my family's history began at age 10 and is now, so far at least, a 40-year-old project. I will be quick to add that I still consider myself an amateur genealogist.

I want to be clear about what I am trying to do in this book – create a good beginning for people new to the world of genealogy. I am drawn to pastimes that demand improvement over time. That attraction worked well for me with genealogy, photography, and chess. There's a reason I don't play golf any more.

A good genealogist never stops learning or developing their methods and techniques. When you don't stay sharp, you set yourself up to hit a brick wall. When that happens, researchers abandon projects or make erroneous conclusions. Mistakes that become part of the "official" record live on to complicate someone else's research.

I can't tell you how many times I hear, "I worked with my family history for awhile and then . . . " or, worse yet, "I couldn't find any proof, but I'm guessing this is right."

For people consumed by the work, a brick wall isn't an insurmountable obstacle; it's a neon sign flashing, "Game on!" If you can't find real proof, the definitive answer has to wait. Sometimes that means years of patience.

Genealogy involves detective work and sound analysis; it should not involve guesswork.

My preoccupation with our family history mystifies some of my relatives. My refusal to accept old family stories as facts frustrates and even angers others.

I proved too much of our personal mythology wrong over the years. I no longer believe stories passed down through the generations. At best, these stories offer clues to the truth. They are rarely accurate.

This whole quest began for me not with a story, but with a photograph given to me when I was 10-years old, a story I share in Chapter 1 of this book. From that day forward, I became that child in the family who loved to sit at the feet of the old people. This proved to be both a rewarding and a frustrating experience at times.

One of my great aunts remained lucid well into her late 90s. She told wonderful stores about her youth, my great-grandparents, and her adventures in the 1920s as a flapper. She was something of a "wild woman" in the family, having married 8 times. I adored her. My many conversations with her are among my most cherished memories.

An elderly second cousin several years her junior lacked that clarity. I loved the old gentleman, but he made my heart sink. "Grandma used to tell me all those old stories about the Civil War, but I don't remember them now." Thirty years later those lost stories still taunt me.

My family's almost legendary longevity allowed me to know several of my great aunts and uncles. One well-loved

second cousin reached the age of 101. She took me to
isolated family cemeteries and told me stories about "our
people." Those narratives included the details of her little
sister's death. The girl died near the turn of the century
when her skirts caught fire, a horrible, but common fate for
women of the time.

I can still hear the sadness in my cousin's voice. "I sat with
her while she was dying, coughing up old black smoke
from her lungs. She was such a little thing to cough so
hard."

Not everyone has the opportunity to hear so many family
stories from the people who lived the experiences. That
generation has now passed. My oldest uncle was born in a
covered wagon. I am writing this on a computer, a machine
not even imagined when he came into this world.

We seldom pause to consider the sweeping historical
changes that occur within a single lifetime. Genealogy will
awaken that new perspective in your vision.

I cannot guarantee that the genealogy "bug" will bite you.
You may read what I have to say and choose to leave the
digging to someone else. Some people love this kind of
research. Others don't even want to talk about the topic.

The fact that you picked up this book at all suggests you
may be in the former category. Make no mistake; compiling
a family history takes both work and dedication.
Regardless of your decision, think of the budding
genealogists that may come after you. Label your family

photos. Take the time to write down the details surrounding a cherished family heirloom. Have a conversation with an older relative and ask for permission to tape the exchange.

You may not become the family historian, but you can prevent the loss of such precious details. For those who do decided to pursue genealogy, prepare yourselves. The experience will be fun, exciting, educational, provocative, and often moving.

Table of Contents

Table of Contents

Free Genealogy Videos

Before I go any further I want to share with a fabulous collection of genealogy videos

Please just visit

www.FreeGenealogyVideos.com so we can email all the videos 100% free – just as an extra 'thank you' for purchasing this book.

The videos cover everything you need...

- Introduction
- Getting Started
- Evernote
- Roadblocks
- Research tricks
- Planning
- And lots more

Make sure you receive them all free at

www.FreeGenealogyVideos.com

Chapter 1 - Why Research Your Family History?

In 1994 sociology professor Robert D. Lambert surveyed the Ontario Genealogy Society. He asked members why they studied family history. This was well before the Internet put a wealth of genealogical information in easy reach.

The top reasons, in order of prevalence were:

- To come to know my ancestors as people.
- For posterity (for children, grandchildren, nephews or nieces.)
- To learn about my roots, about who I am.
- To restore forgotten ancestors to the family's memory.
- A love of solving puzzle.
- To check the accuracy of a family story.
- As a way to study history.

Lambert's research identified other reasons. These had less to do with process and more with the perceived role of "family historian." The position conveyed a sense of authority and "elder statesman" status.

Respondents described taking pleasure from discovering new family information. They enjoyed learning historical and geographical facts. Passing their findings on to an audience deepened that enjoyment.

Many looked forward to interacting with other genealogists at conferences and in online forums. New opportunities to travel delighted them. Some spoke of developing complimentary pastimes like photography or photographic restoration.

Lambert quoted thoughtful and provocative answers to his questions:

- [Genealogy] gives me an anchor in an otherwise very fluid world which is becoming more cold and impersonal all the time, and it gives me a solid foundation, a rock if you will, upon which to build and establish my identity as a person. I am no longer a single isolated entity in a vast sea of humanity - I now have roots and connections.

- I am a descendant of my ancestors and not just my husband's wife.

- Since I likely will have neither money nor possessions to pass on to my daughter, perhaps a genealogy will be my legacy.

- It's amazing to think so little remains of lives lived over a 100 years ago - just a name on a census and a gravestone, but their name is my name too.

Those observations may resonate with you. Your reasons for developing an interest in genealogical research could be unique.

Regardless, one central fact is true. Genealogy demands intense engagement. Using a word like "hobby" almost trivializes the experience.

How I Got Hooked

My love affair with genealogy started with the gift of a photograph when I was 10-years old. I was born late in my parents' lives and as a consequence knew only my paternal grandmother from the previous generation. Some of my first cousins were in their 50s when I was born!

As a precocious child, and a nascent storyteller from birth, the lack of faces to put to names in family stories frustrated me. When my aunts and uncles talked at family gatherings I couldn't see the people they mentioned in my mind. It bothered me.

One Thanksgiving, my Aunt Elizabeth brought me an old sepia portrait affixed to a thick card. As I gazed at the nine people in the photo, she began to explain the image to me, identifying each person by name and relationship.

"That's my mother," she said, pointing to a dark-haired woman cradling an infant in her arms. "And that's my oldest sister when she was just a baby." My interest was immediately pricked. In 1943, that woman died at the hands of her abusive husband, a haunting crime in my family's living memory.

"And this is my father," my aunt said, indicating a tall, strapping man with broad shoulders. "And this is his mother."

I did the generational "math" in my head and asked, with no small degree of wonder, "That's my *great-grandmother*?"

My aunt, a genealogist herself, smiled. "She is, and this is your great-grandfather. He fought in the Civil War even though he had tuberculosis."

These facts weren't new to me. Now they went with the face of a thin man with angular features, a drooping mustache, and a sad expression. "Who is that sitting beside him?" I asked.

"That's his mother."

"My great-*great*-grandmother?"

"Yes, and her name was Elizabeth, too. Her husband died in Mississippi during the Civil War and she lived with

Grandma and Grandpa. I was named for her."

That hooked me in completely. One well-preserved photograph showed me the faces of three generations. It made them "real." That framed picture now sits on my desk.

That afternoon, my aunt took me to my great-great-grandmother's grave. As I stood beside the tall granite tombstone in that country cemetery, I felt connected to the woman buried there.

Forty years later, I visit her resting place when I am in the area. I have a clear mental image of her thanks to the photograph Aunt Elizabeth gave me.

My own mother, who was most definitely *not* bitten with the genealogy bug, often said to me, "Why do you do that? They were all dead years before you were born."

From the instant I saw that photograph, those people were part of my family. I felt as tied to them as I did to the aunts and uncles who sat around our Thanksgiving dinner table that day.

Now that my Aunt Elizabeth has died, I am the one known as the family "historian." My phone rings with calls asking about distant cousins and seeking arcane details about "our people."

The survey respondents were right. I do like the sense of "elder" status that carries, even if I don't like the idea of being old!

Getting Started with Genealogy

Correct and efficient genealogy follows set conventions and protocols. Only corroborated evidence subjected to rigorous analysis should pass to future generations. Nothing else qualifies as a "fact."

In the beginning, proper form will be the last thing you'll be thinking about. You'll want to plunge head first into the details and find out as much as you can. I don't discourage that initial enthusiasm. Have fun, but rein yourself in before you go too far.

If you don't, you'll make incorrect assumptions. Research hurdles will draw you up short because you don't have good notes. You'll have to retrace your steps because you have no idea how you even reached the problem spot in the first place.

We'll discuss documenting your research in Chapter 2. But for now, I want to talk about "get started quick" strategies. These steps will let you enjoy some instant gratification. But they will also give you the necessary information to settle down and get to work.

For your first taste of research, we'll concentrate on basic information. This will facilitate a visit to a genealogical site like Ancestry.com or FamilySearch.org. What you can learn with only a few keystrokes may surprise you.
But after that first "hit," it's time to devise your

organizational structure and to start keeping track of your
work. This isn't as tedious as it sounds. Most genealogists
take great pleasure from analyzing evidence and presenting
well-collated research.

Collecting Your Rough Initial Data

Let's review a few of the things you can do to get started
with solid information. You already know more about your
family history than you realize.

Sit down and make some notes about yourself and your
living relatives. Usually the simple act of writing things
down is enough to begin to jog a person's memory. Include:

- maiden names for female relatives
- places where people have or are living
- the names of children
- occupations
- any dates you remember

Contact other family members and go over your notes with
them. Take down whatever they tell you, even if it conflicts
with your own recollection.

Family stories tend to get "better" in direct proportion to
the number of times they're told. Inconsistencies do have
value. They may offer clues to the real truth behind the
"legend."

Memory is at best, a faulty device, and women have a
tendency to "fudge" their age. You can sort that all out

later. For now, you just need some material on which to base your opening investigations.

Mining the Top Layer of Family "Stuff"

Go through all the family "stuff." What do you have? What is packed away in drawers and boxes in the homes of relatives?

Copy the information, especially photos, with a digital camera or scanner. Ask your relatives to help identify people in pictures. Look on the back of images for any writing.

Don't ignore any kind of relevant scraps of paper or personal collections including, but not limited to:

- birth certificates
- wills
- naturalization papers
- property titles and deeds
- albums, scrapbooks, and baby books
- high school and college yearbooks
- newspaper clippings
- funeral and Mass cards
- Bibles
- letters and postcards
- diaries and journals

If your older relatives are agreeable, set up a time to interview them. (I'd call it "visit with," if I were you. See Chapter 3 for more interview tips.)

Cater these meetings to their level of comfort. Some people clam up in the presence of a tape recorder or video camera. In that case, just have them over for dinner or go to their home for coffee.

Make informal notes and be casual. Older people become impatient if they think you aren't paying attention or listening. Over time, your extended family will accept that you see every gathering as a fact-finding mission!

When you have as much information as you can get from living relatives, get organized and take your research to the next level.

Chapter 2 - Getting Familiar with the Basics

Computers and online resources have completely transformed genealogy. You can still do a genealogy the "old-fashioned" way. Neither the Internet nor software assumes complete responsibility for documenting, analyzing, and organizing data. But these modern tools do make the process much, much easier.

If you are not currently a "computer person," think about becoming one. Technology can take your research to impressive levels. The computer helps to cut down on wasted hours. When you do take a research trip, you'll be more likely to target the information you need.

I love my gadgets and online resources. I will try to strike a middle ground in describing the research process for people who prefer a well-sharpened pencil. But in truth, I am a huge advocate of using the technology to its greatest advantage.

Side Note: Professional / Certified Genealogy

Amateur genealogists spend hours researching their family history for the love of the "chase." In record halls and at microfilm machines the voice of Sherlock Holmes whispers in my ear. "Come Watson, the game's afoot!"

Professional genealogists *live* for the chase. Many are librarians, history professors, or professional archivists. For them, preserving the past is their life's mission.

(You can hire a professional genealogist through many genealogical repositories discussed in Chapter 6. These professionals will help you with research problems for a fee.)

I have not worked with a professional genealogist, but I know two people who have done so with great success. Both faced a complete dead end in their research. The professionals were able to help them get past the problem and find new avenues of inquiry.

To learn more about what professional genealogists offer, and even how to "turn pro," visit the:

- Association of Professional Genealogists at www.apgen.org
- National Genealogical Society at www.ngsgenealogy.org,

- or turn to the near encyclopedic *Professional Genealogy: A Manual for Researchers, Writers, Editors, Lecturers, and Librarians* by Elizabeth Shown Mills.

To explore becoming a board-certified genealogist, visit the Board for Certification of Genealogists at www.bcgcertification.org/certification. The page details the necessary steps for certification, but also addresses the question, "Why Certification?"

What is a Family Tree?

Before I talk about the "modern" tools of the trade, we need to cover the basics of form. What was once a paper-based medium has moved to the computer screen.

I find onscreen family trees to be magical. I'm a visual person and often need to see the whole scope of a family tree to orient myself. This used to mean taping paper sheets together, drawing lines and boxes, and breaking out the thumbtacks.

Now I fill the 27-inch screen of my iMac and ponder generational connections to my heart's content. I will warn you that I think genealogy software only makes this research *more* addictive.

We'll talk about specific genealogy software in Chapter 4. For now, let's visualize what we see in our heads when we hear the phrase "family tree." We've all seen such diagrams from time to time. They look like flow charts, with successive generations linked by lines. You may not realize though that there's more than one way to do a family tree.

Most family trees, especially those compiled with software, incorporate three chart types and include "collateral genealogy." This means the research extends to relatives descended from common ancestors not in your direct line.

This kind of research creeps rather naturally into family tree compilations. No genealogist who discovers information just lets it go! That would be unthinkable.

A fact is discovered and verified about your great-great-grandfather's sister, and you include her in the tree. Then you find out her husband's name. A census records reveals the names of the children. Then you unearth the will detailing the inheritance. One of the sons isn't listed and you want to know why. Welcome to collateral genealogy!

As I've confessed of myself (and I think this is true of many people), much of my love for genealogy lies in the thrill of discovery. The larger my research grows, the better I like it and the better I understand where I came from and how my ancestors lived their lives.

You need to have a good grasp of these standard forms because at one time or another, you will use them all. There are three basic types of family trees: direct lineage, family lineage, and descendant.

Direct Lineage

A direct lineage chart may also be called a pedigree chart or an ascendant tree. That means the "line" begins with you or a person you choose, like one of your parents or grandparents. The chart then follows that single surname or bloodline backwards through multiple generations. This is what most people mean when they make a reference to a family tree.

Family Lineage

The family lineage chart is identical to the direct lineage chart, but the lines for siblings are included. If your father had a brother, that man's wife and children would also be included, as would the siblings for your grandparents, great-grandparents, and so forth. Obviously this makes for a much more extensive chart.

Descendant Tree

A descendant tree works in reverse. You pick an ancestral couple far back in your lineage and work forward, trying to account for all known descendants in both the male and female line.

Finding Family Tree Forms

If your interest in genealogy is new, and you're not yet ready to invest in software, getting started with free printed forms is a good way to find out if this is something you really want to do.

An excellent online source for genealogy forms is Family Tree Magazine at www.familytreemagazine.com/freeforms.

Even if you don't have online access, someone you know surely does and can print out these materials for you. They are offered as Adobe Reader "PDF" files, which is a standard and easily accessible format via free software generally included on all computers, both Mac and PC.

As of this writing in mid-2014, the following categories and forms were offered there:

Basic Charts and Worksheets

- Five-Generation Ancestor Chart
- Family Group Sheet

- Adoptive Family Tree
- Stepfamily Tree
- Relationship Chart
- Biographical Outline

Research Trackers and Organizers

- Personal Records Inventory
- Research Calendar
- Note-Taking Form 1
- Note-Taking Form 2
- Online Database Search Tracker
- Repository Checklist
- Research Journal
- Research Worksheet
- Table of Contents
- Correspondence Log
- Family Correspondence Log
- Article Reading List
- Research Checklist of Books
- Book Wish List
- Surname Variant Chart
- Burned County Records Inventory
- Research Planner and Log

Census Forms

- 1790 Census Worksheet
- 1800-1810 Census Worksheet
- 1820 Census Worksheet
- 1830 Census Worksheet
- 1840 Census Worksheet

- 1850 Census Worksheet
- 1860 Census Worksheet
- 1870 Census Worksheet
- 1880 Census Worksheet
- 1900 Census Worksheet
- 1910 Census Worksheet
- 1920 Census Worksheet
- 1930 Census Worksheet
- 1940 Census Worksheet

Immigration Forms

- Customs List 1821-1882
- Customs List 1883-1897
- Passenger List 1890-1903
- Passenger List 1903-1907
- Passenger List 1907-1913
- Passenger List 1913-1917
- Passenger List 1917-1942

Records Worksheets

- Deed Index - Grantees
- Deed Index - Grantors
- Statewide Marriage Index
- Military Records Checklist
- Cemetery Transcription Form
- Vital Records Chart
- Military Biography Form

Oral History and Heirlooms

- Artifacts and Heirlooms
- Tradition Recording Form
- Time Capsules
- Oral History Interview Record
- Heirloom Inventory
- Photo Inventory

Create Your Own City Guide

- As described on the site, "Use this template to create a customized guide to genealogy research in your US ancestor's town or city. You'll find instructions for DIY-ing your own city guide in the September 2013 Family Tree Magazine."

Don't worry that many of these form titles mean nothing to you now. Browse through them as an educational experience. Print out the ones that both appeal to your sense of organization or that fit your current needs.

For instance, if your interest in working on your family tree has been stimulated by the fact that your mother or grandmother has just died and you are going through her things, the forms for to heirlooms and photos may be especially useful.

I often take printed forms with me on research trips to scribble notes and make rough drafts of theories on which I'm working. Even though I travel with a laptop and a tablet computer, I still do some of my best thinking with pencil and paper.

Because I use genealogy software, I sometimes print data from my files for the same note taking purposes and then go back later and enter the information neatly into the software. This use of charts doesn't take the place of my research log or detailed notes, but rather is my version of a "scratch pad."

But Wait, Isn't Research a Linear Process?

I can almost hear some readers slamming on their mental brakes. "You want me to start by cataloging photographs or doing an inventory of junk in the attic? Aren't I supposed to start with the family tree first?"

Let me try to answer that question by saying that researching your family history is a game of opportunity. One of the best afternoons I spent with my parents before my father's death was going through drawers of old photos and labeling them.

My Dad really got into the process and told story after story. It was fun for us all. I learned many details I'd never heard before. Perhaps because he knew he wasn't going to recover his health, Dad opened up about his childhood, how he felt when his father abandoned him at age 5, what it was like trying to be a "good son" to his mother during the Depression.

Never pass up any opportunity like that afternoon. They don't come back – and never lose a chance to label priceless family photos! It breaks my heart to browse in antique stores and find stacks of photos, some going all the way back to the American Civil War, with no names or other means of identifying the people on the image.

A family's history is being sold as an anonymous trinket for two or three dollars because no one ever took the time to just write a name on the back of the picture! Even if you decide that working on your own family history is not something you want to do, get your family photos labeled while your older relatives are still alive and label your own photos for future generations.

Not everyone in your family will have the same appreciation for clues to the past that will soon be your passion. Heirlooms disappear. Papers are destroyed. And, as heartless as it may sound, the reality is that people die. Always seize the day when it comes to genealogical research. Never count on anything or anyone "being there" when you come back another day.

The phrases "I'll come back and look at that" or "I'll talk with her another day" constitute genealogical sins. One of the greatest tragedies of my personal research is that I never read or transcribed a box of letters to which I had access for years. Out of the blue, my Mother chose to destroy them.

I was absolutely devastated and we had words over the matter. She said, with what was to me maddening matter-of-factness, "Who in the world would care about old letters?" My stomach still constricts when I think about those papers. They are the only documents that would have given me insight into a beloved relative's service in World War II.

Although I confess I was quite angry with my mother, the truth is that I lost that experience because I was lazy. I put off the chore of going through the material and now it's lost to me forever.

As for the linear nature of genealogical research, my advice is to start with what you have and let the information grow as you follow leads, corroborate facts, and verify your data. The straight-line narrative will develop over time, but it's quite rare for the information to fall so neatly in place in exactly that order – in fact, if it does, get suspicious.

When all the material just seems to magically arrange itself, you're likely accepting an incorrect theory and cherry picking the information available to you to fit the scenario you've worked out in your mind. In my experience, easy genealogy is usually wrong genealogy.

Don't try to impose an artificial order on your work and miss interesting and vital information in the process – or accept errors out of the appeal of the path of least resistance. By the same token, don't get so wrapped up on the idea of "doing it right" that you squelch your own pleasure in the process.

So long as you are acquiring multiple sources, analyzing their validity, comparing and collating your data, and establishing proven facts, you're doing it right.

Appended Notes

I assure you that a family history is much more than just a "tree." The longer I've worked with my own genealogy, the more I've come to regard the family tree as a kind of extended visual placeholder. It's extremely useful, for instance, when I'm trying to explain the "how we are related" question to someone.

The real treasures of my own research, however, are the details and stories in the notes I append to each individual's record sheet. (More on that in just a minute.) When I made the transition from a paper-based system to computer records, I spent hours entering all of my appended notes and scanning and attaching documents I transcribed through the years.

Although it was not my intention in the beginning, my research became a loosely written narrative over time and I am now actively engaged in the process of polishing the material for a book.

To some extent all genealogists find themselves learning about the communities in which their ancestors lived and the larger events in which they took part. For instance, it's always important when searching through census records to look at the people living on either side of the family in which you're interested, or even those with homes on the same street.

Later in this book I will describe a project I undertook with a friend to answer a medical question about the potential for inherited cardiovascular issues. Our primary focus was the paternal line, but because her birth father literally disappeared, we were casting a wide net and looking for connections in any community where he had an association, including her birth mother's hometown.

We could not locate the mother's family in online sources, but the surname was everywhere in the town! I called the cemetery and asked the custodian to run a record search for me. He found the graves, which gave me the dates I needed, but then he said, just casually, "You should speak to Dr. Williams. She wrote the town history."

I called the woman, told her my story, and she said, "Oh yes. I know that family." As it turns out, my friend's grandparents were the black sheep in a prominent and entrepreneurial clan of Italian immigrants. When we bought a copy of her book, there were the faces of my friend's great uncles, aunts, and cousins in an authenticated, published record. Needless to say, it was an extremely exciting day for her!

Because my academic training is in the area of history, a subject I taught for a time, I naturally seek out this kind of information. Many new genealogy enthusiasts put on blinders and look for nothing but material on their family. If you don't learn about where your people lived and the events they lived through, you will never really get a sense of them as real people.

This kind of understanding often comes from old family stories that seem charming or even funny at first glance, but actually carry the potential to tell you a lot about how your ancestors thought and felt.

I will hasten to say that no old family tale should ever be taken as a fact at face value. Many things go wrong in such stories. Details from both sides of the family become blended into one story, events that are chronologically far distant become merged, or embarrassing revelations are prettied up so the scandal does not get handed down to future generations.

Listen to the stories, but always verify the "facts" before you make them part of the genealogy you're building. Let me give you an example. I know that my maternal grandfather voted for Franklin D. Roosevelt in 1932 because he told one of my aunts how he cast his ballot, a detail she recorded in her journal entry for that day.

During Roosevelt's second term, my grandfather suffered a stroke and could no longer speak. My mother, who was a teenager at the time, remembered her father sitting by the radio listening to FDR's "Fireside Chats." Though largely mute, Granddad would bang his fist against the table, shake his head, and mutter the one word he could enunciate clearly, "NO!"

Based on one written primary source (a journal entry recorded by a witness at the time the event occurred) and a first person account of my grandfather's behavior (also a primary source) I can say with 90% certainty that my Granddad did not vote for FDR in 1940 or at least did not agree with the progress of the Democratic New Deal to that point in time.

Why am I not completely certain? I don't know if:

- He voted for FDR as the lesser evil because American entry in World War II was almost certain.
- If he did indeed cast his vote. I do know he was registered to vote, but I have no record that he exercised that right.
- If he voted for Republican Wendell Willkie.

But still, what I do know gives me far more insight into my grandfather's politics than I might otherwise have been able to surmise.

Individual Record Sheets

One huge advantage of working with genealogical software is the ability to keep individual notes and records per person. This is also true of many online genealogy services like Ancestry.com.

The individual record sheet (or file or log or whatever you choose to call it) helps you to create an additional layer of order in your research. The sheets also allow you to isolate and keep track of unanswered questions like the ones I investigated around the story of my grandfather's allegiance to FDR and the New Deal.

Software programs typically make it possible for one piece of information to be attached to two or more individuals. So, for instance, if three brothers bought a piece of land together, your scanned image of the deed of sale could be attached to each of their individual records.

This type of thing is somewhat more cumbersome when you are working with paper-based research, but it is essential to associate key information with the people to whom the data relates. This is how patterns emerge and theories are formed.

The All Important Research Log!

At the same time that you should collate your research regarding individuals, all of your work should also fall under the umbrella of some kind of comprehensive research log. Don't fall into the trap of thinking, "Oh, I'm just piddling around with this family tree thing. I don't need to keep a record of what I'm doing." Yes, you do. Trust me

The purpose of the research log is to keep track of sources you've already examined and the information you did or didn't find there. Think of the log as your diary of your research from the planning stage through completion.

Unless you track where you've been and who or what you were looking for while you were there, you will wind up wasting time duplicating your efforts — or worse yet, having to recreate your trail to find a needed piece of information that you didn't write down but vaguely remember. (I speak from personal experience on this one.)

In addition to keeping your research log, it's imperative

that you label your notes with both the date and place, and the citation information for the resource you're reading.

(We'll talk more about citations later. This is one area where your software can take away much of the procedural pain!)

Never think of multiple notations of citation details as needless duplication, but rather as a "back up" system to ensure you get what you need. (If you still take notes on paper, be sure to date and number your pages so they don't get mixed up later.)

Many people use a spreadsheet format for their research log (or have access to this format in the genealogy software they use.) The most basic data field/columns to include in such a record are:

Document Number

All documents stored in archival systems have some kind of reference / location number attached to them. If you have to come back and look at the material again in the future, that number is invaluable. But even if you are working with private documents, create some numbering or ID system of your own to help you keep track of the materials.

I once found myself looking at ledgers in a wool warehouse. My ancestors were ranchers. I was investigating their expenditures for feed during a devastating drought to understand how the family got through the disaster.

No one kept any sort of journal, but when I compared the amount they spent trying to keep the animals alive to what they received for the harvested wool and mohair, they clearly existed on the narrow edge of poverty.

The handwritten records were kept in large leather-bound ledgers in a storeroom of the warehouse. Since I found the ledgers in chronological order, I carefully replaced them that way (always think about the researcher who may come after you!)

In my research log, I was then able to note the documents as "Ledger 1 - Page #" with a fair degree of confidence that if I had to come back, I could return to the material in question easily. (Given the inch-thick layer of dust on the books, the chances they were going to be moved any time soon wasn't all that high!)

Date (Of the Research)

The date entered in the log should be that on which the research itself was performed, not the date of the document you are examining. While this may not be crucial for physical records, the date you looked at the material has relevance for online sources where databases change over time. If a database received a large infusion of new material after you last checked it, looking again is not a waste of time and is, in fact, a very good idea.

Repository

The repository is simply where the item you are examining is stored or located. In the example I gave above under Document Number, I entered the name of the warehouse to which the ledgers belonged. If you are looking at a document on a big online repository like Ancestry.com, that is what you should write down in this column or space on your form.

Original / Extract / Abstract / Transcript

Recording whether you are examining an original record, extract, abstract, or transcript is absolutely crucial because it speaks to the quality and likely reliability of the material itself.

- **Original records** are distinguished from the other "derivative" records because they are, as the name implies, the actual document regardless of type or form. Clearly this is the best and most accurate record to which you can have access. When we discuss citations in greater detail we'll also consider the matter of "primary" and "secondary" information as genealogists use the terms.

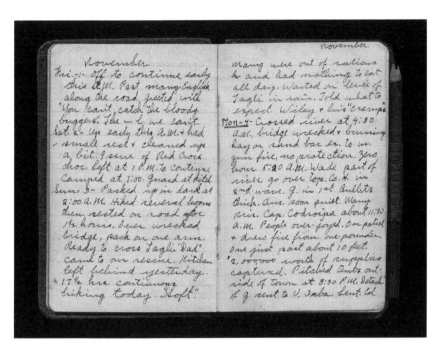

- A **transcript** is a word-for-word complete copy of an original document just as it appears including mistakes. Any interpretations for comments not present in the original are included [like this] in square brackets.

  Transcripts entered digitally into genealogy software carry the added benefit of being searchable.

- An **abstract** summarizes the essential details of a document and includes vital details (name, date, place, events) in the order in which they appeared in the original document.

- An **extract** is only a portion of an original document that is an exact word-for-word copy as in a transcript. Extracts, especially if they appear in other works or are included in other documents are set off by quotation marks.

Analysis

Use this space for very brief thoughts you may have on the information, its quality, readability, or usefulness in answering or posing a question.

(I often use different colored ink if a new question has come to mind based on what I just read.)

Obviously this is not the place for extensive notes, but simply a short means to recall to your mind later your experience (success or failure) with a record or record set.

Link

The link column applies to online sources only, but do use this convention rather than relying on your browser's bookmark feature. Bookmarks get out of hand quickly and I have never found a really good way to keep them organized and accessible to my satisfaction.

Organization is the Point

All of the information in this chapter is intended to illustrate the need to coherently organize your genealogical research in some way. While there are standard conventions for charting, citing, and recording data, I'm certainly not going to suggest there's only one way to organize material.

Even though the bulk of my research resides in computer files, trust me, I couldn't live without sticky notes! You have to do what makes sense to you and what helps you to see the "bigger picture" of your research. But you do have to have some kind of "system."

By starting off with an organizational structure in place, you will save yourself a huge amount of time and you will be able to use and share the information you do locate more efficiently.

If your research grows to the point of my own personal project so that composing a narrative family history becomes your primary objective, these records and notes will form the basis of your manuscript. You want them in the best possible shape!

I've been able to transfer whole paragraphs from notes on individual record sheets over to my manuscript with the magic of "copy and paste," with only minimal rewriting.

For more information on arranging and keeping well-organized genealogical research and records see:

- *Organizing Your Family History Search* by Sharon DeBartolo Carmack

- *The Organized Family Historian* by Ann Carter Fleming

Please note that Sharon Carmack's book, which appeared in 1999, is out of print, but can be located at used bookstores and on Alibris.com.

The Matter of Paper Documents

No matter how extensively you may work with genealogy software or how faithfully you create digital images of the records you acquire, as a genealogist, you will ultimately be drowning in paper, everything from certified copies of official documents to stacks of family photos.

In order to learn how to preserve and protect these materials, I suggest you begin with the book *How to Archive Family Keepsakes: Learn How to Preserve Family Photos, Memorabilia and Genealogy Records* by Denise May Levenick (Family Tree Books, 2012.)

Although none of us particularly like to contemplate our own deaths, give a thought to what will happen to all of your genealogical materials when you die.

If no one in your family is interested enough to preserve the information or continue the work you have begun, consider donating your collection to a local or regional museum or historical association. If you don't think to the future of your work, the sad truth is that relatives who do not share your passion for the past may throw it all away.

Even if you are lucky enough to have a family member who will gratefully inherit your work, think about copying your materials and presenting them to the same institutions. It is important that your findings become part of the accessible record that will be at the disposal of future genealogists. Having benefited from the personal files of my fellow researchers, including published family histories, I am a huge advocate for these types of donations.

Chapter 3 - Working with Living Relatives

As you begin your research, you should plan to visit with your older living relatives and to learn as much information from them as possible. For this reason, I want to talk a little bit about interview techniques and "etiquette." If you make the mistake of just putting a recording device in front of Great Aunt Ethel with directions to, "talk about the family," you probably aren't going to get very far.

Also, don't go into the experience looking for facts only. Older people like to tell their stories without being interrupted. Be respectful and listen to their meandering "tangents" with interest. They'll likely reveal all manner of tantalizing leads. Be sure to take notes of names, places, and events. You can verify specifics later.

Avoid all open ended "yes" and "no" inquiries. Prepare your questions in advance, but don't feel you have to work through them all — just have material ready to jumpstart the process as necessary.

I will confess that I genuinely like the company of old people and am fascinated by their opinions and recollections — even when they're grumpy or force me to drink endless cups of tea. Sometimes having a degree in history has actually been a great blessing in these encounters.

After a dear friend's grandfather suffered a stroke, the sweet old gentleman tended to wander around in time a bit. I used to visit him in the nursing home and admired the way he tried to keep up with world events by faithfully watching the news every day. The 2000 presidential elections were going on in the United States, but Dan kept thinking Franklin Roosevelt was running for office.

We'd sit and talk about the New Deal and the Depression until he'd waft back in and refer to George W. Bush as "the president's boy," (his reference to George H.W. Bush), which was my signal to shift to the present day.

In the process of keeping this slightly addled old fellow company, I learned exactly how he felt about the politics of the 1930s and heard many of his stories about being a young man working with the Civilian Conservation Corps.

Although he couldn't remember what he had for breakfast that day, he reeled off dates and place names with perfect confidence. I took that information and cross-referenced it to records pertaining to CCC projects and rosters and was able to verify when he signed up and where he worked. He had been absolutely correct on every single point he told me.

When I shared these details with his granddaughter, she said, "Granddaddy would never talk about the CCC! That is so cool that he told you that!" She was also touched by his ability to accurately recount the details of this period of his life. It meant the intelligent, quick-witted man she knew and loved was still in "there" somewhere within the confused place his present-day mind had become.

I share this information with you as a gentle admonition to be patient — and kind. You may be dealing with elderly relatives who have no other audience for their stories. Let them enjoy themselves and pay attention to what they say. With elderly people, long-term memory is often crystal clear no matter how significant their degree of short-term memory loss.

Devices or No Devices?

Obviously it is to your advantage to record interviews either with an audio or video device, but be forewarned that some people absolutely clam up under these circumstances. You may be forced to rely on written notes, at least for the first interview.

In the following two sections, I talk about copying photos and documents with a digital camera and a computer tablet. While I realize that not everyone owns these devices, where practical to do so, they are indispensable investments in the success of your genealogical work.

While both devices are excellent for making copies during the course of visits with older relatives, they can also be used in a wide variety of settings for collecting and collating original materials.

Copying Photographs

It is quite common that relatives will show you old family photographs while you're talking. If you have a small digital camera on hand, you can easily copy the images. For that matter, you can use the camera in your cell phone if the resolution is high enough (5 megapixels or greater so the images will print well if you so desire.)

Here are some copying tips from my own experience

- Don't use the flash on your camera or phone.

- Place the image to be copied on a flat surface and direct a light on to it. Desk lamps work well for this purpose, but make sure there are no glare spots on the image or glass if the photo is framed.

- Stand over the image and try to hold your camera as level as possible. If you hold the camera or phone at an angle, the people in the image will be distorted.

- Make sure that you are not casting a shadow over

the image.

- Be sure to focus the camera and take multiple shots of the image. I generally take a minimum of three.

In your written notes, record a description of the image and take down the names of the people shown as well as the date and location if known.

Clearly there is nothing difficult about this technique, but it does take some practice. Make trial shots of your own photos, both color and black and white, so you can copy images on site quickly and efficiently.

Old people can be very protective of their family photos. Be as non-invasive and non-threatening as possible in obtaining workable copies for your own records.

I've been pleased with my own efforts in this kind of photo preservation. The digital images are easily shared and I've printed and framed many copies of photos that otherwise would be far too fragile to display and enjoy.

Copying Documents

For copying documents, you may want to use a small portable scanner, although some cameras do have settings for photographing documents. My own solution for document scanning is to use an app on my iPad Mini. Taking the small tablet with me is much less cumbersome and I've found the quality of the scans to be excellent.

Although there are many such applications in the Apple iTunes store, the one I have used with great success is Scanner Pro. (Go to readdle.com to watch a video demonstration of the application.)

There are also scanner applications for Android tablets, although I have no direct experience with them. I suggest that you use your favorite search engine and look for "best scanner app for Android." Read reviews and try out some of the free applications on your own documents to find one that works well for you.

Formulating Your Questions

An excellent source for getting ideas about questions to use in interviews is the Story Corps website at www.storycorps.org. If you've never heard of this effort, the group has been collecting and archiving interviews since 2003. To date, they have amassed more than 50,000 conversations that have been added to the American Folklife Center at the Library of Congress.

Story Corps is one of the largest oral history projects of its kind, with ongoing scheduled sessions around the United States. If you or a loved one is interested in participating, you can use the site to book an appointment when the group is in your area. (Please note that if you book an appointment and cancel, there is a $50 cancellation fee.)

The project runs a number of special initiatives, including (but not limited to) the Memory Loss Initiative, StoryCorps Alaska, and the September 11th Initiative.

(For a similar effort in the United Kingdom, please visit the website of the Oral History Society at www.ohs.org.uk. Under the section on "Advice" there is a page entitled "Practical Advice: Getting Started" with many excellent tips.)

Under the Story Corps site's "Record Your Story" section, there is a selection of "Great Questions." These are some of the suggested questions for Family Heritage, which I am paraphrasing and augmenting:

- Where is your Mom/Dad's family from?
- Did you ever visit there as a child/adult?
- What was that like?
- Did you know your grandparents?
- What do you remember about them?
- Do you remember any of the stories they told?

- Were there stories told over and over in the family?
- Did your Mom/Dad have brothers and sisters?
- Did you know/visit with them?
- Who were your favorite relatives?
- Did your Mom/Dad have a favorite joke? song? book? movie?
- What did your Mom/Dad do for a living?

Focus on questions that will elicit long responses. Get in the habit of repeating bits of information to cue the person to provide more detail. For example:

- Your elderly aunt says, "I was a cheerleader when I was in high school in 1925." You answer with, "Wow, what were the cheerleading uniforms like back then?"

- Your Grandmother's statement, "My sisters and I went to school in a one-room school house," might elicit a response like, "How did that work with so many grades in one room?"

If a topic comes up and you don't know enough to ask more, make a note to do some research for a second interview.

In one-room schools the older children often helped out with things like carrying in firewood or giving the younger kids a hand with their lessons. In a follow-up conversation you might say, "After we talked, I read more about how one-room school houses worked. Did you have chores to help the teacher? What was she like?"

Even if you know the answer to a question, ask it anyway. You may learn interesting things including topics the family likes to avoid. In my own research, an aunt-by-marriage told me one of my mother's sisters gave birth to a child out of wedlock in the 1930s.

When I worked up the courage to ask Mother about it, her response was, "She shouldn't have told you that." The fact that Mother did not, however, deny the story confirmed for me that it was true, which I was later able to verify through official records.

Don't underestimate the amount of detective work that is required in genealogy. Sometimes what you *aren't* told is more important than the information supplied openly!

I will say, however, that discretion is often the better part of valor. Some questions are best not put out for discussion if a painful family secret is clearly involved. I was in my twenties at the time this incident occurred and frankly, I handled it poorly.

If that information were passed on to me today, I would not ask my mother, but would instead go straight to the records. My mother and her sister-in-law didn't speak for three months after my impolitic question. I highly recommend not starting a family feud if at all possible!

Handling Sensitive Topics

Since my own family history involved a murder witnessed by the deceased woman's sister and son, I was put in the delicate position of interviewing them together about the events of that day.

There are no hard and fast "rules" for this kind of situation, but I will share what I did to prepare for the interview. I gathered as many newspaper records as I could find and reviewed all the "official" details.

Because I lived nearby, I visited the house where the killing took place. I knew, from having heard the story many times, the rough sequence of events. This allowed me to "walk" the crime scene so I had a picture in my head of the setting.

When I sat down with my relatives, I said. "If I may, let me tell you what I understand happened that day. Please interrupt me to add or correct anything you like." I started with the facts and in just a few minutes, I was playing witness to a detailed joint narrative of that awful day. I stopped talked and listened, making note of everything that was said.

Excruciating details emerged that allowed me to reconstruct the killing in a chilling, step-by-step fashion. To my great shock, my cousin even recalled his mother's last words.

There is an interesting addendum to this story. Many years later my phone rang one day. A tentative and apologetic voice on the other end of the line identified the caller as the murder's nephew. In his family, no one was allowed to tell the story, which had become a dreaded and black secret.

He asked me if I would tell him what happened. I did, and although it was devastating for him to learn about what his uncle had done, the facts also gave him a great deal of relief. The entire family had assumed a burden of guilt that was not theirs to carry.

In that moment, I was extremely grateful for my long-time genealogy "obsession." It allowed me to give a family comfort years after a tragedy that my own people had always taken as strictly "ours," forgetting how many individuals were touched by the events of that day.

Although the details will be different, I can promise you will run into some topic that your relatives consider sensitive in some way. No matter how much you want the facts to complete your research, be sensitive to the emotions involved. Realize that you may have to go to other sources to get the definitive "last word."

Neither my mother nor my cousin could remember the time of day the killing occurred. My mother thought it was in the morning. My cousin insisted it was about noon. They were both in agreement, however, that the town doctor was summoned immediately.

It was only when I tracked down the death certificate that I was able to learn my aunt was pronounced dead at 5:30 in the afternoon. This time was corroborated by the incident report in the files at the local sheriff's office. The shock of the killing was so great that time had no meaning for the other people who were there that day.

I took this verified information back to my mother and cousin. My mother remained adamant that the time was wrong, but my cousin recalled the way the rays of the setting sun slanted across the front yard as he sat on the front porch steps in the aftermath of the killing. He said he could not go back in the house where the crime scene was being cleaned up because the sight of the blood was too much for him.

Interviews about emotionally charged, sensitive topics can be extremely difficult and painful, but they have a tremendous power to connect you with the deepest experiences your family has endured and overcome.

Chapter 4 - Genealogy Software

Truthfully, I think that anyone interested in really maximizing their genealogical work today should have a computer and access to the Internet. The amount of information that can be accessed in just five minutes will astound you. Think I'm kidding?

The Family History Library in Salt Lake City, Utah is the largest genealogical library in the world. Their holdings are massive and impressive:

- records for more than 110 countries, territories, and possessions
- more than 1.6 rolls of microfilmed records
- access to more than 2.4 million microfilmed records
- 727,000 records on microfiche
- 356,000 books and serials
- 4,500 periodicals

- 3,725 other electronic resources

For your reference, the complete contact information for the library is:

> The Family History Library
> of the Church of Jesus Christ of Latter-Day Saints
> 35 North West Temple Street
> Salt Lake City, UT 84150-3400
> Telephone: (801) 240-2331
> Fax: (801) 240-1584
> E-mail: fhl@ldschurch.org

If you visit the library's online presence at FamilySearch.org and go to the "Learning Center" you will find a series of five-minute introductory videos on getting started with genealogy.

The first video challenges you to locate a specific record for one of your ancestors in less than five minutes. When I was writing this book, I tried it, using only my grandfather's name.

In 2.5 minutes, I was looking at a copy of his death certificate — a digital image of the real document, not a transcription. Having done genealogy "the old-fashioned way," I can assure you that is nothing short of astounding — not to mention time saving!

So, what software should you buy?

Researching any kind of technology product can be an

exhausting process. There are certainly more than three genealogy programs out there, but I have chosen to discuss Family Tree Maker, My Heritage Family Tree Builder, and Legacy Family Tree because they are consistently ranked as the top three programs in this category.

If you want to read more reviews I highly recommend this site, GenSoftReviews at www.gensoftreviews.com.

One of the most important considerations with this type of software is the ability to work with the GEDCOM file format, an acronym for "GEnealogical Data COMmunication."

When you wander out of mainstream programs like the ones I will discuss below, file format can become an issue. To understand more about this critical issue, I recommend the following article by Kimberley Powell from About.com:

"Genealogy GEDCOM 1010: What Exactly is a GEDCOM and How Do I Use It?" at genealogy.about.com/od/family_tree_software/a/Genealogy -Gedcom.htm

Family Tree Maker 2012

Family Tree Maker 2012, produced by Ancestry.com, is widely considered the best software for both beginners and experienced genealogists. Due to the enhanced integration with the Ancestry site via the "TreeSync" feature, this package neatly bridges the gap between online and offline genealogical work. The affordable $39.95 price tag, plus a

Chapter 4 - Genealogy Software

free trial-period with Ancestry.com only enhance the software's attractiveness.

The program's web dashboard allows users to search online data without having to go through a web browser. Search results integrate with the software for specific information, minimizing the need for manual entry. Adding media to your family tree is simple with integrated scanner support and the ability to download directly from Ancestry.

For more advanced researchers the GPS/Latitude-Longitude feature allows you to build a digital map showing prominent locations in the lives of your ancestors. Maps may be added to family trees to more clearly show geographical distraction and migration patterns.

Reviewers point to numerous other tools included in the program including timelines that plot major life events including, but not limited to, education, occupation, marriage, and migration.

A relationship calculator makes it much easier to determine how any two people on the tree are related, and the global spell checker verifies the accuracy of all names and place names even in foreign languages. There are a full slate of options to create reports, charts, and even books to be shared with other family members.

Family Tree Maker consistently garners top marks for ease of installation and use, customer support, and value for the purchase price.

www.FreeGenealogyVideos.com   P a g e | 59

My Heritage Family Tree Builder 7.0

Although Ancestry.com has gained a reputation as the online environment to build your family history, there are many other vibrant and thriving genealogical communities, including MyHeritage with more than 33 million users! The site's Family Tree Builder, now in its seventh edition, is available for download completely free.

There is, however, one catch. Some of the features are only accessible in the premium version, which can only be unlocked if you pay $75. Is it worth it? Devotees say yes, and the software has been downloaded almost 6 million times.

The site and software support more than 40 languages.

Building a media-rich family tree with the software is a highly visual, involving just a few mouse clicks. The process gets positive feedback from reviewers for user friendliness and solid results.

There are, however, many things you'll want to do that you can't without paying for the software. When you buy Family Tree Builder, you also get a premium subscription to the site, which includes online publication of your family tree and associated media on a dedicated family site.

The SmartMatch module takes sections of your tree and matches them up with trees uploaded by other members to automatically expand the included research. There is a smilier record matching feature that goes out and looks for additional historical records that are connected in some way to the one you're currently viewing.

This is also the only genealogy software on the market with face recognition technology to enhance the tagging of uploaded photos. Data online and off syncs fully, and, like the Ancestry site, you are part of a large genealogy community at MyHeritage.

Legacy Family Tree 7.0

Legacy Family Tree 7.0 is affiliated with FamilySearch.org, the online presence of the Family History Library in Salt Lake City.

Like Family Tree Builder, there is a standard edition for free, while the deluxe version costs $29.95 for download and $39.95 if ordered on a CD. While the core features are very similar to those discussed in the other two programs, the Legacy SourceWriter is a stand out addition to this software. It helps researchers with proper citation to sources according to the accepted genealogical standards.

Many researchers overlook the citation process because they find it arcane and confusing, or make up their own way of indicating the origin of their information. Accurately referencing sources is a critical part of genealogical work that should never be ignored. Legacy Family Tree definitely takes the pain out of that process.

Making Back-Ups

Regardless of the genealogical software with which you choose to work, always ensure that you have a method for backing up your files, either online in one of the "cloud" services like Dropbox or in a physical format.

Personally, I do both. Standalone external hard drives are relatively inexpensive and come in configurations large enough to back up all your genealogical files. Those files that are scanned or copied with a digital camera may be quite large, so make sure you purchase a drive with adequate space.

You can purchase an external drive with a TB (terabyte) or more of space for less than $200. If that means nothing to you, a drive with 1 TB is sufficient to hold approximately 800 full-length feature films. That should more than accommodate your genealogical files.

Once you have your materials safely stored on an external drive, I recommend storing that drive somewhere other than your home or securing it in a fireproof box. Set a schedule to perform regular backups and follow it religiously.

If you come into a large collection of papers and spend several days scanning and copying the data, make a special backup of the new material just in case anything goes wrong while you are integrating the new files into your existing genealogical records.

Chapter 5 – Considering the "Paperwork"

For me, personally, genealogy software tames the "paperwork" monster, the foundation of all such research, but also the complete bane of everyone who takes up the quest for a family history.

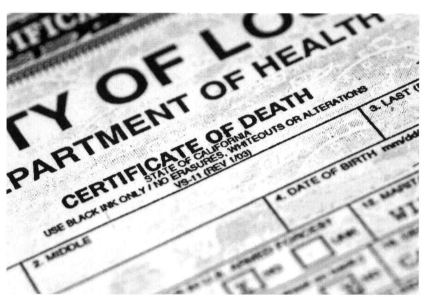

The computer does not, however, free you of understanding the nature of the data you're using and the correct way to "fill in the blanks."

Primary vs. Secondary Sources

We've already considered the difference between an original and a derivative record and talked about transcripts, abstracts, and extracts. All information derived from such sources can be categorized as:

- **Primary**, meaning set down by someone with

firsthand knowledge of the event in close chronological proximity to the occurrence itself.

- **Secondary**, recorded by someone with secondhand knowledge of the event, and/or chronologically at a distance from the event itself.

Information is said to be "**indeterminable**" when the relationship of the informant to the information cannot be determined. The accuracy of facts from indeterminable sources certainly carries a diminished perception of reliability. In these cases, try to confirm the material from another, more verifiable, source.

Sources vs. Evidence

Understand that sources provide information, which provides evidence of three types: direct, indirect, and negative.

- **Direct evidence** is obvious. It answers your research question on its own with no need of corroboration

- **Indirect evidence** must be combined with another piece of evidence to provide an answer.

- **Negative evidence** is used to create an interpretation or conclusion about a research goal because information you might expect to exist can't be located.

As a general rule of thumb, you should have two

independently created pieces of evidence in your possession that both provide the same "answer" before you regard that point as a "fact."

(Depending on the quality of the sources, three or more may be required to truly prove your theory.)

Recording Information

Whether entering information into a computer program or filing out a paper form, these are some of the basic and accepted conventions for data entry.

Names

Enter names in the natural or "normal" order: first, middle, and last (surname.)

John Henry Smith

For married women, use the last name with which they were born (maiden name). If you wish to record both names do so in the following way:

Jane (Smith) Jones

The maiden name appears in parenthesis before the married name. This form is often used in narrative family histories

Some genealogists capitalize the entire last night: JONES. This method makes the name stand out on paper family tree charts, but is not recommended for use with genealogy software.

There are many naming conventions that exist for special cases, all of which are handled by the top software packages, but let's look at a couple of examples.

If a woman has been married several times, her name is written as shown above, but the married names are given in chronological order of husbands:

Jane (Smith) Jones Adams Thomas Moore

If the same woman had a nickname, it would be given as:

Jane "Jay Jay" (Smith) Jones Adams Thomas Moore

Look for special alternate name fields in your software for these and other difficult naming problems.

Dates

Dates must be recorded with great care, especially by genealogists working in the United States because Americans use a different order for dates than most of the rest of the world: month, day, year

July 4, 1776

To avoid confusion, use the international format, which is: day, month, year.

4 July 1776

Write out the name of the month to ensure complete clarity. If you are uncertain about a date, it can be entered as either "about" or "circa" in the following manner:

abt. 1890 or c. 1890

If a date is uncertain, but has been narrowed to a range, use between:

> bef. 4 July-15 July 1776

It's also an accepted practice to use "before" and "after" in chronological references:

> bef. 4 July 1776 or
> aft. 4 July 1776

The guiding principle is to be as specific and clear as possible in providing all chronological references. Always remember that someone may come along in the future and augment your work. Make sure you provide them with good data!

Place Names

Like references to dates, place names should also be highly specific, working from the smallest to the largest jurisdiction in the following order:

- town, village, city
- county or parish
- state or province
- country

For instance:

> Boston, Suffolk County, Massachusetts, United States

Source Documentation

Understanding and correctly entering the factual data you find clearly stands as one of the pillars of well-conducted genealogical research. Citations, however, are just as fundamental to this type of work because they verify the accuracy of the material for anyone who might choose to check your findings, and allow someone else to go to that same source to further their own research.

The citation standard for genealogical work is *The Chicago Manual of Style*, which calls for the inclusion of the following components:

- author (or whoever created or supplied the data)
- title (including title of websites)
- date (either publication or creation)
- location information (for instance page or entry)
- details of publication (place, publisher, and date or repository and location

This is how that data might look for one of the books I used in my research for this text:

Powell, Kimberly. *The Everything Guide to Online Genealogy: Trace Your Roots, Share Your History, and Create Your Family Tree*. (Fairfield, Ohio: Adams Media, 2014), pp. 32.

There are many, many forms of publications and documents that you will be called upon to cite, many more than I can enumerate here. Each calls for a specific placement order of elements.

I highly recommend the "QuickSheet" guides at the website Evidence Explained (EvidenceExplained.com), as well as the book *Evidence Explained: Citing History Sources from Artifacts to Cyberspace* by Elizabeth Shown Mills.

Most genealogical programs will format citations for you when you enter the required information, and many of the online resource sites supply you with the fully formatted citation at the bottom of the page.

For the purposes of illustration, I went to FamilySearch.org and did a random search for the name "John Smith."

The first record on the list was a citation to a head of the house from the 1940 census. At the bottom of the abstract of the record, the citation was provided in full as:

> United States Census, 1940," index and images, *FamilySearch* (https://familysearch.org/pal:/M M9.1.1/VRZF-72Q : accessed 26 Sep 2014), John W Smith in household of Hilda Smith, Dover, Representative District 5, Kent, Delaware, United States; citing enumeration district (ED) 1-8, sheet 8B, family 188, NARA digital publication of T627, roll 544.

Not only are detailed citations of use to genealogists who may one day pick up your work, they also serve as your "bread crumbs."

If you ever have to go back and look at a source again, a complete citation makes it much easier to go straight to the record you need. It will only take one long, boring, repeat search in an archive looking for a record you "know" is there to convince you of that fact! For as tedious as citations may seem, they are crucial!

Standards of Excellence

The benchmark for excellence in genealogical research is strongly represented by the work of the National Genealogical Society founded in 1903 in Washington, D.C.

Because I regard the group's Standards For Sound Genealogical Research so important, I am producing them verbatim from the Society's site at www.ngsgenealogy.com.

Genealogical Standards

Standards For Sound Genealogical Research Recommended by the National Genealogical Society

Remembering always that they are engaged in a quest for truth, family history researchers consistently —

- record the source for each item of information they collect.

- test every hypothesis or theory against credible evidence, and reject those that are not   supported by the evidence.

- seek original records, or reproduced images of them when there is reasonable assurance   they have not been altered, as the basis for their research conclusions.

- use compilations, communications and published works, whether paper or electronic,   primarily for their value as guides to locating the original records, or as contributions to the   critical analysis of the evidence discussed in them.

- state something as a fact only when it is supported by convincing evidence, and identify the   evidence when communicating the fact to others.

- limit with words like "probable" or "possible" any statement that is based on less than   convincing evidence, and state the reasons for concluding that it is probable or possible.

- avoid misleading other researchers by either intentionally or carelessly distributing or   publishing inaccurate information.

- state carefully and honestly the results of their own research, and acknowledge all use of   other researchers' work.

- recognize the collegial nature of genealogical research by making their work available to   others through publication, or by placing copies in appropriate libraries or repositories, and   by welcoming critical comment.

- consider with open minds new evidence or the comments of others on their work and the conclusions they have reached.

Chapter 6 – The Online Big Three and More

Genealogical resources literally abound online. There are thousands of sites, most with simple interfaces that allow you to begin your research with just a few mouse clicks. Options to share your findings with family and friends and to connect with others genealogists make the research even more appealing, exciting, and addicting.

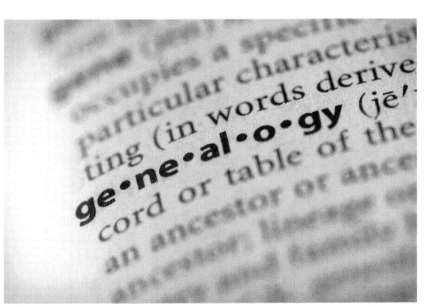

Frankly, it's incredibly easy to get overwhelmed and lost unless you have a good idea about where to start. In this chapter, I've decided to tackle what I regard as the "Big Three" of online genealogical sites: Ancestry, MyHeritage and FamilySearch.

These sites include information forms we've already discussed (transcriptions and abstracts) as well as indices and images.

- An index is simply a list of names that may include

relevant facts like date and location that serve to direct the researcher to original documents.

- Images are the online equivalent of original documents. They may be presented as either image or PDF files and are of equal research value (and validity) as the original piece of paper from which they were created.

When genealogical material first began to appear online, most data was in the form of an index. Now, however, original documents are quickly catching up in scope and volume and it's possible to do an amazing amount of your research from the keyboard of your own computer.

When original documents are not available online, the information that can be accessed generally provides the necessary references to locate the original housed in a courthouse, archives collection, or other type of records repository.

In many cases, contact can be accomplished via email, including the process of filling out a request form to gain a certified copy of the document.

Ancestry

There's no sense arguing with the assertion that Ancestry.com is the biggest player in the online genealogy game, or at least the best known thanks to their generous advertising budget. Still, the diversity and ease of use the site offers, including 29,000 searchable databases and more than 13 billion records is hard for any competitor to rival.

With a single search, users can comb through birth, marriage, death, immigration, census, court, school, military and many other record types in multiple countries. Since the collection is updated on an ongoing basis, it's not unusual for members to receive Ancestry "hints" (little green leaves) to indicate new connections through which they can expand their research on a daily basis.

After a 14-day free trial period there are monthly and annual subscription prices. A U.S. Discovery Membership at the time of this writing in mid-2014 was $155.40 for a year and $22.95 per month. An annual World Explorer Membership was $299.40 or $34.95 per month.

(Please note that the UK version of the site can be found at www.ancestry.co.uk.)
In addition to being able to build and share your family tree

online with attached multi-media elements, Ancestry is also home to a large family history community where members discuss their findings and help one another over the inevitable research hurdles.

The site's learning center has good information for beginning genealogists, including a direct link to downloadable paper forms if you prefer to "Start with Paper and Pencil."

The videos "First Steps #1: Getting Started at Ancestry.com," "First Steps #2: Tips for Successful Searches," and First Step #3: Now What? How to Use Your Discoveries to Make Your Next Big Find" offer a good introduction to working with the site.

Much more in-depth information is available under the "Next Steps" tab, and there is an introduction to the Ancestry community under "Our Social Network."

I am an Ancestry user and have had good luck with the site on a whole. This is not to say, however, that I have not had to go outside the massive Ancestry database to find information to augment my family tree. Since it's easy for users to upload images and append notes, groups of even distant relatives can get to know one another quickly.

Since I have been working on my family tree for many years, and have been fortunate enough to have been given numerous old photos, I've passed those on to relatives in digital form via the Ancestry database and have received, in return, access to personal documents and images I never knew existed.

Ancestry is not cheap, but if you have the budget to accommodate the subscription price, the site is well worth your time to the point of being addictive. I have not yet opted to have my DNA tested, one of the newer Ancestry offerings, but I am contemplating the idea. You can learn more about the $99 service at dna.ancestry.com.

MyHeritage

MyHeritage.com does not have its own name databases, but relies instead on a comprehensive search engine that simultaneously accesses more than 1,526 databases including census, immigration, military, medical, cemetery, court, and land probate records as well as newspapers, telephone directories, and family trees.

The online community of users is regarded as a corollary resource. It's common to see links posted to family trees, historic photos, and public family websites. This is a very socially driven research community, which is what attracts many of its users - more than 75 million of them by 2010.

In 2013 MyHeritage entered into a strategic partnership with FamilySearch that brought billions of records within the site's search potential. In February 2014, the company teamed with BillionGraves for a global initiative to preserve the world's cemeteries. By April 2014, it was estimated that users could access more than 5 million historical records in 40 languages.

Although MyHeritage is free, a paid subscription ($6.25 per

month for Premium, $9.95 for PremiumPlus billed annually) allows users unlimited storage space and removes ads from the browsing experience.

Basically this service is a mixture of research and social networking, and it does compete quite favorably with other sites in terms of depth of research and ease of use — a capacity that continues to grow. However, if you don't want the social interaction, MyHeritage is not for you.

FamilySearch

The material, tools, and educational resources available at FamilySearch.org are presented free of charge by the Church of Jesus Christ of Latter-Day Saints, which also maintains more than 4,000 family history centers around the world.

There are fewer digital images and documents on FamilySearch than on other sites, but the digitization process is ongoing and catching up with the competition at a steady pace. (Some links currently take users out to Ancestry, where a fee may apply for use.)

Everything on the FamilySearch site is free, including family tree and pedigree download. This policy reflects the underlying LDS philosophy that families are a central aspect of our lives.

As an example of the scope of the available data, users have access to the Ancestral File database, which contains 36 million names referencing pedigree charts and family group records submitted to the Family History Department since 1978.

The International Genealogical Index and its addendum contain an aggregate 725 million names extracted from marriage, birth, and christening records or submitted by patrons. An additional 380 million names are contained in the Pedigree Resource File.

A robust search engine accesses census lists, court and legal records, family histories and genealogies, land and property libraries, and vital records as well as data from

- cultural and religious groups
- key genealogical sites
- migration sources
- royalty and nobility

- surname and family organization

Most of these categories can be narrowed by state or country in addition to other search criteria.

Reviewers give the site commendable marks for ease of use while admitting that sometimes it can be difficult to find the document you need with the search interface.

In my experience, this is usually a product of entering too much specific information. With FamilySearch, I recommend starting with a single piece of information (your ancestor's name) and gradually adding facts until you find what you want.

One of the strongest aspects of the FamilySearch site is the Learning Center, which is packed with excellent video tutorials to expand your understanding of genealogical work.

While I would not recommend relying solely on FamilySearch, I think a free membership to this site should definitely be a part of your research arsenal.

Other Online Genealogy Sites

There is absolutely no way to provide short summaries for all of the genealogical resources available online. I don't even mean to suggest that the following material does more than skim the surface.

Basically I've selected these sites because, like cream, they tend to rise to the top of review lists for this genre of content. Like all things online, they can be bumped off those lists by newer or more comprehensive offerings at any time.

Archives.com

Archives.com, launched in 2009, offers an affordable option for genealogy enthusiasts who might be priced out of some of the other subscription sites. Its features, however, are highly competitive when measured against even the biggest player in the game, Ancestry (including the recent addition of DNA testing.)

Standard membership costs $39.95 per year and provides full access to 269 searchable databases with more than 1.6 million records, including 300 million U.S. vital records. The digital repository of more than 120 million scanned newspaper images stands out as a unique and highly useful feature.

Unlike many other sites of this type based in the United States, Archives includes 290 million UK census records and 160 million UK vital records, both including document images.

Beyond that, however, the remainder of the international data is limited to about 14 countries total, making the global scope of the site much narrower than that of the competition.

For a fee, Archives will send staff members to retrieve

courthouse records for subscribers, and facilitates (for an additional fee) the ordering of birth, death, marriage, and divorce document copies.

Archives makes family tree integration with Facebook simple, and leverages the networking power of the social media site, which is quickly becoming a center of regional based genealogies to gather and exchange information on their pages.

Reviewers like the clean and simple organization at Archives and praise the intuitive power of the integrated family tree charting.

The customer service and help functions consistently score top marks and there is a 60-day money back guarantee. If you use Archives.com and you're not happy with it, the company will refund your money.

World Vital Records

WorldVitalRecords.com operates from a highly location-based point of emphasis. If, for instance, you know that your relatives are originally from Italy, your search can be narrowly targeted for the applicable record sets.

Pricing is competitive at $39.95 for an annual U.S. Collection membership, while a World Collection membership is $99.95. Regardless of which you choose, you may use the site for seven days free of charge to try out the features. Members also receive a monthly genealogy newsletter.

The World Collection membership gives users access to:

- all U.S. and international records including those

from the UK, Ireland, and Canada
- access to more than 1.4 billion names worldwide
- content from partner sites like Newspaper Archives and Genealogical.com among others

Available records include, but are not limited to vital, census, court, immigration, and military records as well as newspapers, family histories, and family trees. This includes access to more than 8,000 yearbooks from high schools, colleges, and military units.

MyTrees.com

MyTrees.com contains a database of existing family trees made up of more than 280 million names, one of the largest "pedigree linked" collections online. In addition, the site encompasses 64 other record collections with more than 250 million names. These include, but are not limited to:

- federal census records
- Social Security Death Index
- U.S. Civil War records
- U.S. naturalization records
- U.S. Revolutionary War pension application file names

There are only a few international records, principally from the United Kingdom, Canada, and New Zealand. Unfortunately they are not complete and are most extracts, which detracts from both their accuracy and perceived value.

Other resources available through MyTrees.com include, among others, the services of professional genealogists, white pages for locating living relatives, free forms, and tools to assist with digitizing photographs and slides.

Reviewers are complimentary about the ease of searching the site, but point out the limited utility of help options. Users can only get telephone support to pay a bill or with a technical issue, but emails are answered within a 24-hour period.

Mocavo Plus

Mocavo, which debuted in 2011, is actually a genealogy specific search engine designed to query only genealogically relevant sites. The free version is available to all visitors, but there is a paid option called Mocavo Plus, which offers more complex search options including:

- first name alternatives searches
- intelligent date searching
- date ranges
- geo-searching
- and exclusions, among others.

The stand out aspect of Mocavo Plus, however, is that it focuses on content that is available free of charge, including the same kind of birth and death records available on subscription sites as part of the monthly or yearly fee. Mocavo looks for free sources of the same information like sites built by local volunteer genealogists.

While this may sound like a great potential cost saver, I do want to inject a word of caution. When you look at material presented on free sites, you are generally seeing either abstracts or transcripts. Both are highly subject to error.

If you find facts through Mocavo that provide the necessary evidence to prove a genealogical theory, you should then progress to viewing the original document. That is the only way you'll be able to absolutely confirm that you have accurately proved your assertion.

Reviewers are not complimentary about Mocavo's customer support, pointing out that the company is only a couple of years old. If, however, the Colorado-based endeavor wants to stay competitive in a people-oriented niche like genealogy, this is an area in which they will need to show consistent improvement.

Although the site is relatively easy to use, if you opt to pay for Mocavo Plus, don't expect to get much in the way of help. For this reason, I can really only recommend Mocavo for users with strong pre-existing search skills.

Genealogy Bank

Most of the data available at Genealogy Bank, an offering by NewsBank, Inc. is derived from newspapers dating back to 1690. Depending on your research goals, this point of emphasis can be a strong positive or completely useless.

If you are willing to invest the time and interest and already have a reasonable amount of information about your family, this site can be a good place to find more obscure facts about your ancestors.

Although some critics regard newspapers as weak and deeply biased sources, these publications exist to chronicle daily life in a community. It is from the pages of newspapers that you will learn about your ancestors' social lives, their participation in local affairs, their membership in clubs and other organizations – even what kind of lace a bride chose for her wedding veil.

Published obituaries often provide a wealth of information about an individual's role in the life of his town. You may find out to what fraternal lodges he belonged, and what men served as pallbearers at the funeral.

This type of information is much more intimate than the contents of the "official" record and goes a long way toward fleshing out the bare and often sterile bones of a genealogy.

Genealogy Bank is an excellent resource for ancestors in the United States, but will offer no help on those from another country. All told, the site includes content from 5,800 newspapers. The content has been scanned, so you are seeing the original source material.

Additionally, Genealogy Bank makes available local histories, biographies, directories, land grants, orphan petitions, military pension requests – even funeral sermons. Frankly, it is a fascinating place to just browse. I've managed to get completely and happily engrossed there on more than one occasion.

The interface is simply, straightforward, and logical, with good tips available on in the "Help" and "FAQ" (Frequently Asked Questions) section. There is an "Ask the Genealogist" page and site staff can be reached by both phone and email.

OneGreatFamily

OneGreatFamily approaches genealogy from the perspective of a global project to unite all the research of people who join the site. This creates a sense that the overall endeavor is a shared research project.

The member family trees are interwoven in the hope of creating a great "universal" tree, thus proving the name of the site itself – that mankind is indeed "one great family." It is certainly an interesting approach and one that can yield good results under the right circumstances.

When a member enters new information in the site, the interface determines if that data already exists or whether it conflicts other existing data. The appropriate users are then notified, allowed the researchers opportunities for collaboration and resolution of the identified issues.

This is not a site to which I would send people just beginning to discover information about their ancestors, but it is a resource for taking a well developed family tree to see if the connections can be linked farther back in time.

Users can view literally hundreds of family trees and their associated documents like photographs, scanned records, and even video clips.

The quality of the database and the accuracy of the provided content depend entirely on the users. The site does make resources and tools available including a surname index, learning center, and newsletter archive.

Formatting Better Searches

No matter how much the Internet has become a part of everyday life for most of us, either on our computers or smartphones, the truth is that the vast majority of people have no earthly idea how to really use a search engine.

Regardless of where you are searching for your ancestors — with Google or Bing or on a major genealogy site — there are basic conventions that will vastly improve your results.

Know Details? Use Them

If your great-grandfather is named John Smith and you type just that into any search engine, why would you be shocked that *your* John Smith isn't the first one on the list? Take the basic facts that you know about any relative and narrow your search with simple details:

John Smith doctor San Antonio Texas

Your John Smith still may not be the first one on the list, but you'll stand a much better chance of finding your great-grandfather. If you're looking for something specific, try adding that:

John Smith San Antonio Texas obituary

There are also a number of search "operators" that are useful in tightening the focus of your queries.

Search Operators

Search operators work in all of the major search engines and allow you to fine tune your results with much greater control than just typing in words and phrases and hoping for the best.

When you type in a phrase, the search engine looks for the words regardless of where they appear on the page or in what order. Enclose the phrase in *quotation marks* — "John Smith" — and the search engine will look for the exact phrase.

Most search engines assume the use of the Boolean operator *AND* when you enter two words, but putting **OR** between words can be extremely useful in searches. (Both AND and OR must be in all caps.) An OR search might look like this:

John Smith OR Smythe

The use of this operator lets you search for your relative incorporating any alternate spellings of his or her name.

Search engines exclude small, extremely common words like "and" and "the," but if you have a word that must be included in your search, you can force the engine to look for it by using the **+** *sign*:

John Smith+will

This technique does not work with Google, which discontinued the use of the + sign after launching Google+. The same search in Google would look like:

John Smith "will"

The addition of a *minus sign* in a search tells the engine to exclude that word. This is especially good if your ancestor happens to have the same name as a famous person or even a product.

In her book *The Everything Guide to Online Genealogy*, Kimberly Powell uses an example for this operator that I just love:

> Jimmy Dean - sausage

Formatted this way, the search engine will exclude results for the Jimmy Dean company, like their breakfast sausage.

I also like the command *site:* which restricts your results to one site you specify. The website for the National Archives is www.archives.gov, so if you enter the following search, the engine will look at that site only for that exact name:

> "John Smith" site:www.archives.gov

Not all search engines use the same format conventions for their special operators and advanced techniques, so always find the "help" page for the engine you're using and find out what you can and can't do to improve your search results.

Cyndi's List

No discussion of online resources would be complete without reference to a near encyclopedic starting point for genealogical resources of all types, Cyndi's List at www.cyndislist.com.

The site contains more than 320,000 links and is organized

into 199 categories including, but not limited to:

- Adoption
- African-American
- Beginners
- Biographies
- Births & Baptisms
- Books
- Cemeteries & Funeral Homes
- Charts & Forms
- Citing Sources
- Databases
- Death Records
- Diaries & Letters
- Dictionaries & Glossaries
- Directories: City, County, Address
- DNA, Genetics & Family Health
- Education
- Ellis Island
- Evidence Analysis & Evaluation
- Family Bibles
- Female Ancestors
- Genealogy Standards & Guidelines
- Handwriting & Script
- Heirlooms & Keepsakes
- Heraldry
- Hit a Brick Wall?
- Immigration, Emigration & Migration
- Land Records, Deeds, Homesteads, Etc.

This is just a small sample of the wealth of information on the site. The links are constantly updated. In the category for "Libraries, Archives & Museums" alone there are currently 9,572 links! Cyndi's List is as close to a genealogical "one-stop" shop as you will be able to find.

I especially commend to you the section on Education, which, at the time of this writing in mid-2014 contained 217 links subdivided into the following categories:

- Audio and Video from Conferences
- Awards, Competitions & Scholarships
- Campus Classrooms
- Conferences, Seminars & Workshops
- Correspondence, Independent, and Home Study Courses
- Credentials: Certification and Accreditation
- General Resources
- Online Courses & Webinars

It is completely possible to hone your genealogical skills with online study courses you can finish at your own pace in the comfort of your home. I encourage everyone involved in genealogy to engage in this kind of ongoing training. The more you learn, the more successful you will be at creating a complete and compelling family history.

Chapter 7 – Common Mistakes to Avoid

Lists seem to be the "in" thing in information delivery. Understandably, any traveler setting out on a journey appreciates signposts along the way.

I read all manner of "top" compilations of things not to do as a beginning genealogist and had a private laugh over having been personally guilty of pretty much all of them.

Relaying Exclusively on Favorite Sources

Getting comfortable with one or two sources can lead to a dangerous degree of complacency and limited vision. Many beginners look only to birth and death records and the census to find the bare bones of their family lineage.

Make no mistake; all are excellent sources of information, but with limitations. If, for instance, a child is born out of wedlock, no father's name will be listed on a birth certificate.

Erroneous assumptions can be drawn from census records. For instance if a husband is listed in one census year, but is absent from the next, most beginners will assume the man died in the intervening period, but without a death certificate or probate records, there is no proof of that fact.

I knew one researcher who was absolutely certain her great-grandfather died in a given year because she found a receipt for a tombstone. She later found out, however, that he purchased the marker and carried it with him in the back of a wagon to his new home in Texas. The man lived 20 years past the date when she was certain he was dead!

In the 19th century men often went ahead of their families to build a home or to establish a business in advance of a family migration or took jobs in other areas during hard times. A "missing man" might simply have been living elsewhere when the census was taken.

In her book *The Family Tree Problem Solver: Tried-and-True Tactics for Tracing Elusive Ancestors,* Marsha Hoffman Rising relates the story of Christian Newcomer of Manor Township, Lancaster County, Pennsylvania. Due to unsubstantiated "connections" to his offspring based on names only, 72 children were attributed to this man in various genealogies over the years!

When you rely on a limited pool of records, many things can go wrong including, but not limited to:

- confusing people with the same or similar names
- asserting incorrect "facts" about an individual's fate
- assigning children to the wrong parents

This is why consulting and comparing many different kinds of documents to substantiate a fact or set of facts is fundamental to the genealogical process.

Falling in Love with a Theory

Falling in love with a theory is a little like falling in love with a bad boy. You know he's not the guy for you, but you date and/or marry him anyway. (And then wonder why you wind up in divorce court!)

What typically happens when you craft an elegant theory that explains a genealogical snarl is what I like to call "evidence bending." This leads you to say things like, "Oh Elizabeth Smith and Lizzie Smith *have* to be the same person."

No, they don't. I have a grandfather whose given name was "Alf," not Alfred. While it's true that his name could have been incorrectly set down on a record, the only safe assumption you can draw is that your theory is *wrong*, until you have multiple sources by different authors that prove otherwise.

Making Excuses for Conflicting Record

You cannot escape the fact that old records contain errors for the simple fact that human beings created them! You should not only expect misspellings, but also be open to the fact that people change their names. A woman named Sarah may decide she likes "Sara" better, or an Ann may add an "e" and become "Anne."

By the same token, however, don't assume a discrepancy is a mistake. You may be looking at two different people. These are the cases in which a broader understanding of an individual's circumstances lends clarity.

A man listed in a census as a day laborer is not going to be the same man who leaves a generous landed estate to a group of heirs three years later even if they do have the same name and live in the same county.

"Oh! I Want to Be Related to Him!"

In genealogy, you always start with a known fact and work backward to the next verifiable known fact – you don't jump over four generations with scanty evidence because you just *know* you're related to some famous or otherwise desirable figure.

Beginning genealogists who give into this desire can take absolutely fantastic logical leaps to "prove" they are correct no matter how laughable their "evidence" may be. My best advice to you is to get those stars out of your eyes!

Everybody finds someone remarkable in their family tree, even if that person is not present or lauded in the history books. You may find a relative who aided runaway slaves on the Underground Railroad, a great-great-grandmother who worked for women's suffrage, or a man with no education who worked hard and put his six children through college.

Embrace the people to whom you are related. Don't waste your time trying to create kinships where none exist.

Studying Documents in Isolation

Many beginners treat historical documents as if they exist in isolation both from the people who created them and from the broader record. You must compare and correlate the information in multiple documents to approach any genealogical question from all angles. No other method will allow you to successfully reconcile conflicting data.

This involves as much analysis as you can realistically apply to the potential motive for the document to exist. Always ask yourself if the behavior or event chronicled in the document consistently matches other known facts about your ancestor.

No matter how certain you may be that a single document proves a fact about your ancestor, verify that fact with at least one more document from another source. Don't fall for the trap of the magic document that answers all problems.

If you examine every document you locate and correlate the information you find, you will discover the real magic that lies in piecing together the story of your family's past where one fact always leads to the next logical question.

Take a Shotgun Approach to Surnames

Some researchers operate on the assumption that every person with the same last name is related and essentially take a shotgun approach to gathering records. They copy every single thing they find with no thought to establishing connections and wind up drowning in a sea of facts and paper with no connecting links to tie it all together.

Remember, and this cannot be said often enough, work backwards from a known fact creating one proven link after another. Don't just look at the people that have the "right" last name.

Also, become familiar with the people with whom your family associated. Because groups of people often migrated together, you may have to look for a known associate to pick up the dropped thread of evidence on your own family.

Other Red Flags

In addition to these mistakes, all of the following are potential pitfalls you should work to avoid in analyzing both historical documents and old family stories:

- **Embellishments**. This happens frequently with

military records (privates and lieutenants have an odd habit of becoming colonels over time) and with monetary wealth and social standing.

- **Historical impossibilities**. If you've been told that your relative participated in two major historical events, make sure that it is both chronologically and spatially possible for that person to have been in both places.

- **Inconsistencies**. In my own family history, I was long told that my great-great-grandfather was a colonel in the Confederate army and served in Kentucky – until an independent source led me to the discovery that he ran a saloon in Texas during the war.

- **Compound errors**. The supposed Confederate colonel in the point above? The colonel part came from an embellishment perpetrated by his daughter who tried to get a Civil War pension after her father's death by claiming he was an officer when, so far as I can tell, he didn't serve in the war at all.

- **Omissions due to embarrassment**. These kinds of mistakes are generally created intentionally to hide divorces, crimes, affairs, or illegitimate children.

Always hold yourself accountable for the quality and accuracy of your research. Remember the fellow with the supposed 72 children. You do not want to be part of creating those kinds of roadblocks over which future genealogists will stumble and fall!

Chapter 8 – Research in Action

Having read many books on genealogy, I know how easy it is to take a "how to" approach and in the process, completely lose people -- or create the impression that there is only a single way to get information. Far from it! Genealogical research is all about thinking outside the proverbial box, getting creative, and "free styling."

To disabuse you of the notion of "one right way," and to illustrate how one person's family search began, I asked my friend Patsy to allow me to tell the story of our research into her unique genealogical problem.

It Started with a Specific Question

After Patsy's doctor fussed at her about her cholesterol levels, the physician asked, "Is there a history of heart disease in your family?" Patsy, who was adopted at age 9, couldn't provide a complete answer.

Several years earlier she located her birth mother and acquired some basic health information from her, but Patsy's father, who abandoned the family when Patsy was just 6 was a complete unknown.

Patsy came to me and said, "Do you think we can find out anything about my birth family, especially my father's side?" I asked what she knew about him, and she gave me his name. That was it. She'd never even seen a photo of the man. Needless to say, it wasn't much to go on.

Where to Start?

Before her adoption, Patsy went through a series of foster homes. She shared a report from Child Protective Services with me that detailed some of the circumstances of her early years. There was scant information on the absent father, but I found a brief reference to his having had a minor brush with the law. That was the opening we needed.

With only a name, a location for the incident, and a vague sense of when it happened, we started at Newspapers.com. This is a site that I do use from time to time, but I don't maintain a constant subscription. At $79.95 a year, I think it's a little pricey, but the per month cost of $7.95 is reasonable when you just need the material briefly to work out the kind of problem Patsy and I faced.

The site includes more than 3,300 newspapers across the United States from the 1700s to the 2000s. Out of respect to Patsy's privacy, I won't divulge the family name, but it was as common as Smith or Jones and just as difficult to track down in the absence of dates or other particulars to narrow the search.

Our initial investigations yielded nothing useful, so we made the decision to do things the old-fashioned way. We started going through every edition of the newspaper in which we suspected the police report would appear for the year when we believed the crime happened.

It was a long and tedious chore, but in the end we found two separate stories about the incident. One of the articles included a street address, which allowed us to go back to the U.S. Census records and backtrack until we located Patsy's grandparents.

That was actually an exciting development. When I took the information we discovered and entered it on the Ancestry search interface, fortune smiled on us. A cousin Patsy didn't even know existed had already compiled an impressive family tree that worked backward from their common grandmother.

While this was not the information Patsy directly sought, it was still exciting for her to see her lineage outlined from the present day to Scotland in the 13th century with a direct connection to the royal House of Stewart. We learned that her mother's people were from Maryland and had deep roots in the American South.

Returning to the quest for the elusive father, we were now determined to find out where he went after his brush with the authorities, the incident that seemed to help trigger his abandonment of his family. Patsy knew that her mother married her father when he returned from service overseas in World War II, so military records seemed to be our next best bet.

Census records yielded enough rough vital information, including the man's approximate birth date, that we were able to locate his enlistment and service record through Ancestry. Gradually we filled in more and more details about the man's life, but where he went when he left his family remained a total mystery.

The Dilemma of Common Names

Part of the dilemma we faced came from the commonality of her father's name. Just for purposes of discussion, we'll call him John Smith. As impossible as it may be to believe, there were two John Smiths in the last town where we could track Patsy's father, and a third living within a 20-mile radius.

The first John Smith turned out to be a highly decorated African American airman from World War II who was written about in numerous newspaper accounts of the period. He was easy to rule out of our search.

The second John Smith led us on a merry chase, however. Everything about him fit. His movements paralleled those of Patsy's family as we had constructed them. His age was correct. But we could never get the kind of confirmation that would have made me certain. For one thing, every reference to this man's wife read only "Mrs. John Smith."

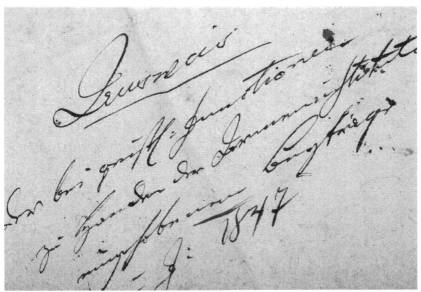

Just at the point that we were ready to contact this man's surviving son, I finally found the wife's name – it wasn't the same as Patsy's birth mother. We had spent weeks on the wrong man and now had no choice but to go back to our last verifiable fact and start over. Welcome to genealogical research!

The Third John Smith

The third John Smith took us out of 1962 and moved us forward to the mid-1980s where we placed him in a nearby retirement home prior to his death. Could he be Patsy's father?

With no other viable avenue, we contacted the home, which

was still in business, and learned that this John Smith was buried in a pauper's grave in the adjacent cemetery. Because the home had taken down the information when he checked himself in, the death certificate we requested included his parent's names.

The data was a match to the couple we had already verified were Patsy's grandparents. We had located her father – who died of complications from long-term cardiovascular disease. Patsy had the answer her doctor needed to fine-tune her health care and to safeguard her from the effects of a potentially inherited predisposition for similar issues.

Did the Project End There?

Even though Patsy's genealogy was technically "finished" in relation to the question that began our project when she found out about her birth father's health, she was bitten with the bug.

Frankly, my friend is competitive by nature, and all the missing pieces in her new family history drove her crazy – like the identity of her paternal great-grandparents, which proved maddeningly difficult to pin down.

Patsy signed up for an Ancestry account and set about copying over information from her cousin's chart and pursuing the blanks spots in her own direct line.

At the same time, she started researching the genealogy of her adopted family, a close knit and fun loving clan of Italians that immigrated to the United States early in the

20th century.

Her journey with genealogy began with a practical and potentially vital health-related question, but the path to find that answer brought her more closely in touch with the roots of both her birth family and her beloved adopted family.

Because the answer we needed lay with a man who had died in the last 50 years, we used somewhat unconventional detective work to run him to ground. Now, however, Patsy is full tilt into standard genealogical work, combing through the records and assiduously verifying every fact to multiple sources. She's proven to be one of my best students in this regard.

And There Was a Surprise

The real "ending" of this story, however, is the most surprising twist of all. After Patsy's father abandoned his family, he went to the West Coast, married again, and fathered a son.

Patsy stumbled onto a high school photograph of her brother at e-yearbook.com. She told me it was like looking at her own 8th grade school photo. Not wanting to intrude on her brother's life or family, she asked me to contact him and verify the relationship based on specific details we learned in regard to the man's military service in World War II in Europe.

When I reached her brother and discussed theses fact with

him, all the pieces fell into place. He was ecstatic to learn that he had a sister and anxious to talk to Patsy and meet her. What started as a question about her cholesterol culminated in a wonderful new relationship with her brother, his wife, and children.

Chapter 9 - Genealogy Terms

If you are a person with a love of words, genealogy will be a constant delight. For instance, you may not know that there is more than one kind of will, with specific terminology for each variation.

A holographic will is one that has been handwritten and signed by the individual, while a nuncupative will is one that has been dictated or declared to a testator. In some circles this is called a "death bed declaration" and is witnessed and afterwards put into writing.

As a lover of arcane language, learning this kind of distinction is just another of the pleasures of genealogical research for me. The following terms should be taken as a kind of "beginner's glossary."

I still run across words and phrases with which I am unfamiliar, but the longer you work with your family history, the more conversant you will become with the standard "lingo."

A

abstract - An abstract summarizes the essential information from a document and includes details like names, dates, places, and events, presented in the same order as they appear in the original record.

abut – To adjoin or border as in land, estate, or farms. A term often used in land records.

accretion – The right to inherit based on survival.

adoption – The act of taking an individual, usually a minor child, into a family to raise through a legal measure.

affidavit – A statement, either written or oral, made under oath.

ancestor - Any person from whom you are descended, for instance your grandparents, great-grandparents, and so forth.

authenticate - Any means by which a source or document is shown to be real and not a fake or forgery.

authored narrative - This is any kind of source that has been created from information the author has gathered and interpreted.

B

banns - An announcement made in public of a couple's intent to marry, usually issued in a church. A type of marriage record available before the marriage license became common.

base-born – A term indicating that the person in question was born out of wedlock; illegitimate. Also referred to as a bastard.

bondmaid – A female slave also known as a bound servant, one not entitled to wages.

bondman – A male slave also known as a bound servant, one not entitled to wages.

bounty land - Land that is conveyed as payment for military service.

C

cemetery records - Cemetery records include the names of those buried on the site, including death dates, and typically the location of grave sites. Usually these records are kept by the caretaker of the cemetery or by any entity associated with the upkeep of the burial sites, as is often the case in cemeteries where no active burials are taking place. Note that this may be the local historical association.

census records - In the United States since 1790 a census or official enumeration of the population has been conducted every 10 years. This is not, however, the only type of census available to researchers. Some states have or continue to conduct their own census measurements, and other countries have their own schedule of census enumerations.

certified copy - A copy of any record that is created by and attested to by individuals who are in charge or or have authority over the original and can authenticate the accuracy of the provided facsimile.

collateral genealogy - Collateral genealogy is an extension of a direct lineage chart in that it includes information on additional relatives who descend from the same common ancestor.

collateral line - A line of descent from a common ancestor, for instance, a connection through an aunt or uncle.

consanguinity - Consanguinity refers to the degree of relationship between people who are descended from a common ancestor. A father and son are said to have lineal consanguinity (in a line), where as an uncle and nephew have collateral sanguinity.

D

deed – A document to transfer ownership of property.

derivative record - A derivative record is some portion of an original record that has been reproduced, like an abstract, extract, or transcript.

descendant tree - A descendant family tree works backwards (as opposed to the usual pedigree or ascendant family tree) in that it begins with an ancestry couple several generations back and works forward to account for all the descendants in both the male and female lines.

direct evidence - If a piece of evidence is uncovered that answers a research question on its own with no need of supporting information, it is said to be direct evidence.

direct lineage - A direct lineage chart may also be called a pedigree or ascendant family tree. These charts usually begin with a parent or grandparent and work backwards following the single surname or bloodline through multiple generations.

E

emigration - The act of leaving one's own country to live in another.

enumeration - An enumeration is a list of people as in a census.

extract - Extracts contain only a portion of the original document, but are word-for-word copies set off by quotation marks rather than summaries as is the case with an abstract.

F

family group sheet - A family group sheet is a genealogical form that presents information on a single nuclear family (husband, wife, and children.)

family lineage chart - A family lineage chart tracks the direct descent of a given line within a family as well as that of corollary lines derived from siblings in the various generations.

fee simple – An inheritance that is direct and complete with no limitations or conditions on its use.

free man of color – A black man who was free from the time of his birth or was emancipated later in his life.

freedman – A man who has been freed from or emancipated from a condition of enslavement.

freeman – A male who has reached the legal age to vote, to own land, and to practice a trade. Not to be confused with "freedman" above.

G

GEDCOM - GEDCOM, the acronym for GEnealogical Data COMmunication, refers to a particular computer file format that is used by the majority of genealogy programs.

genealogy - Genealogy is the study of an individual's family history or ancestry.

good brother – An archaic term for brother-in-law.

good sister – An archaic term for sister-in-law.

good son – An archaic term for son-in-law.

grandam – An archaic term for grandmother.

I

immigrant - An individual coming into a country from their original country of origin to become a resident.

indeterminable information - When the source of information cannot be determined it is said to be "indeterminable," and therefore carries less perceived accuracy.

indirect evidence - Indirect evidence is information that has to be combined with other material to answer a question that arises during your research.

L

land records – Deeds that prove ownership of a piece of land by a particular individual.

late – A term indicating that the person in question is deceased.

legacy – Property or money left to someone in a will.

lineage - A lineage is a line of descent that can be traced directly from an ancestor.

loco parentis – Latin for "in place of parents."

M

maiden name – A woman's last name before her marriage.

majority – A person who has reached legal age.

manumission – The act of releasing an individual from a condition of servitude or slavery.

marriage bond – A document obtained prior to marriage affirming that there is no legal or moral reason why the wedding should not take place. Also an affirmation on the part of the man that he can support both himself and his new wife.

maternal line – A line of descent traced through the ancestry of the mother in a family.

mulatto – A person who, for legal purposes, is considered to be of mixed white and black heritage. In some instances also used to refer to people with Native American blood.

N

naturalization records - The documents that record the process whereby an immigrant becomes a citizen in their new country.

nee – Denotes a maiden name; Ann Smith nee Jones.

negative evidence - When you come to a conclusion or create an interpretations based on information that is absent, you are using negative evidence.

O

octoroon – A child whose parent was a "quadroon," or one-quarter black, making the child one-eighth black in ancestry.

of color – An archaic term referring to a person who is African American, Indian, or of mixed blood.

Old Dominion – In the United States, a traditional reference to the state of Virginia.

oral history - A collection of family stories transmitted in an oral form that are either transcribed or recorded in some fashion.

original record - As the name implies, an original record is the actual document pertinent to your ancestor's history, for instance a birth or death certificate or a marriage license.

P

paleography – The study of handwriting, often crucial in genealogical work to decipher documents.

parish – The ecclesiastical jurisdiction or division of a church, or a reference to a specific church.

pension – A military benefit paid for a person's service or disability as a consequence of service.

primary information - Primary information (or evidence) is any information that has been provided in any form at the time of the event by a person who has firsthand knowledge

primogeniture – The right of the eldest son to inherit his father's entire estate to the exclusion of younger sons and any female relatives.

progeniture – A direct ancestor.

S

secondary information - Secondary information (or evidence) is provided by someone who has only secondhand knowledge of the facts or information and has recorded them some time after the event itself occurred.

sic – A Latin term that is used to indicate that a copy of a record reads exactly as the original was written even in the presence of a mistake.

source – Any record, document, manuscript, publication, or the like that is used to prove a fact.

statute – A law.

surname – A last for family name, for instance, Smith or Jones as opposed to a "Christian" or first name of an individual.

T

transcript - A transcript is complete, word-for-word copy of the original document.

V

vital records - Records that track the major events in a person's life like birth, marriage, and death.

W

will - A document that outlines how an individual wishes their business to be settled and property to be distributed upon their death. The process by which these instructions are carried out is referred to as "probate."

Acronyms

The following acronyms or abbreviations are among the most common you will encounter in your genealogical research:

AAGG: African-American Genealogy Group

AAHGS: Afro-American Historical and Genealogical Society

ACPL: Allen County Public Library in Fort Wayne, Ind.

AGBI: American Genealogical-Biographical Index

AAD: Access to Archival Databases (part of NARA's Web site)

AIC: American Institute for Conservation of Historic and Artistic Works

APG: Association of Professional Genealogists

ARC: Archival Research Catalog (part of NARA's Web site)

BCG: Board for Certification of Genealogists

c., or ca. – The abbreviations for "circa" means about or around.

CG: Certified Genealogist

CGL: Certified Genealogical Lecturer

CMSR: Compiled Military Service Record

CWSS: Civil War Soldiers & Sailors System

DAR: Daughters of the American Revolution (also NSDAR: National Society, Daughters of the American Revolution)

ED: Enumeration District, a geographical division defined for a US census

FEEFHS: Federation of Eastern European Family History Societies

FGS: Federation of Genealogical Societies

FHC: Family History Center , a branch of the Family History Library

FHL: Family History Library in Salt Lake City

FHLC: FHL Catalog

FOIA: Freedom of Information Act

FTM: Family Tree Maker genealogy software

GAR: Grand Army of the Republic, a network of organizations for Civil War Union veterans

GEDCOM: Genealogical Data Communication, the computer file format for family tree data (.ged is the extension for these files)

GLO: Bureau of Land Management General Land Office

GPS: Genealogical Proof Standard

HQO: HeritageQuest Online genealogy databases, offered through many libraries

IAJGS: International Association of Jewish Genealogical Societies

ICAPGen: International Commission for the Accreditation of Professional Genealogists

IGI: International Genealogical Index

ISFHWE: International Society of Family History Writers and Editors

ISOGG: International Society of Genetic Genealogy

LOC: Library of Congress

MRCA: Most Recent Common Ancestor, the most recent ancestor you share with another person

NARA: National Archives and Records Adminstration

n.d. – An abbreviation used in many records to indicate

either "no date" or "not dated."

NEHGS: New England Historic Genealogical Society

NGS: National Genealogical Society

OR: The Civil War reference The War of the Rebellion: A compilation of the Official Records of the Union and Confederate Armies

PAF: Personal Ancestral File genealogy software

PALAM: Palatines to America

PERSI: Periodical Source Index to family history articles in US and Canadian magazines and journals

RM: RootsMagic genealogy software

SAR: Sons of the American Revolution

SCGS: Southern California Genealogical Society

SCV: Sons of Confederate Veterans

SGGEE: Society for German Genealogy in Eastern Europe

SMGF: Sorenson Molecular Genealogy Foundation

SUVCW: Sons of Union Veterans of the Civil War

TMG: The Master Genealogist genealogy software

UDC: United Daughters of the Confederacy

WRHS: Western Reserve Historical Society, Cleveland, OH
Specialized Dictionaries and Glossaries

A Glossary of Archaic Medical Terms, Diseases and Causes
of Death
www.archaicmedicalterms.com

Glossary of Old Occupations and Trades
genealogy.about.com/library/glossary/bl_occupations.htm

Historical Dictionary
www.historytoday.com/dictionary

A Web of Specialized Online Dictionaries
pessoal.sercomtel.com.br/assis/English/Dictionaries/www.y
ourdictionary.com/diction4.html

Afterword

In writing this book, I've tried to give you a solid foundation to take your first steps toward building your family tree. However, I've also shared many personal anecdotes and I hope useful insights. There was a point to all of this that goes beyond my natural tendency to tell stories.

Sometimes it's easy to forget that genealogy is about people, not about musty sheets of paper in a records room or digital facsimiles online. If you don't connect with the humanity of your ancestors in some way during this process then yes, I do think you're "doing it wrong."

This was the point I was never able to get across to my own relatives who could not understand my interest in "people who died before you were born." It did not stop them from coming to me with questions, but they certainly did not share my passion for unearthing the details of our shared ancestry.

My take on this aspect of genealogy may be a romanticized notion on my part, but it isn't one I'm prepared to give up. Let me try to explain why – by telling you another story. After years of working on my family's story, a cousin many times removed sent me scans of my grandmother's autograph book.

On the pages of this girlish treasure, penned in a careful hand, I found a shy love note from the boy who became my grandfather. For many years before I ever knew the autograph book existed, I looked at their wedding picture with fond amusement.

Granddad was the epitome of a gawky farm boy with the most enormous ears and the biggest Adam's apple I've ever seen. The expression on his face in the picture is equal parts terror and delight.

His young bride wears the same determined expression evident in all of her pictures well into old age. She holds his hat in her hand and looks into the camera with steady resolve. Together they look like what they were, a couple of country kids starting a life together.

In addition to the wedding picture and the scans of her autograph book, I have his pewter inkwell, a remnant of his few years of education in a one-room schoolhouse. When I look at the inkwell, I can now imagine him composing those painfully sweet letters to the girl he married and with whom he had nine children.

Thanks to my own birth order in the family, I never knew my grandfather, but through my research and with these relics of his life, I have managed to build a connection with him that has created a sense of relationship. To my surprise, I can truthfully say I love him and am proud to be his granddaughter.

Given the online resources and learning materials available today, it is possible for anyone to sign up for an account at a site like Ancestry and to begin working on a family tree immediately. The speed with which a genealogy can begin to take shape is, frankly, amazing.

Even though, as I hope I've made clear, there are many research standards and conventions you should learn, there is a lot to be said for "diving in" as my friend's story in Chapter 8 makes clear.

After her immediate goal was met -- discovering what health problems led to her birth father's death – she found relatives she never dreamed existed and connected with them. Hers was a positive outcome. She was welcomed with open arms.

In our haste to resolve those issues, we made mistakes that had to be corrected later, but neither one of us regretted the decisions we made together or how we pursued the relevant information.

For me, it was an amazing experience to watch someone discover her family. I've always joked that you can't throw a rock and not hit someone I'm related to. When we began, she had never even seen a photo of her birth father.

Regardless of the degree to which you choose to preserve your family history, my best advice is to have fun with it. Learn to laugh at what you find. I discovered one of my distant relations burned down a courthouse before he could be hanged as a horse thief!

Though it may sound entirely too philosophical for some, genealogy has the capacity to give a person a new grounding in the world. I am the last of my direct line, but it's hard to feel "alone" knowing all the people who came before me. I have set down the record and I know that when I am gone, our story will not be lost.

Regardless of your motivation for finding your own ancestors, I wish you the best of luck, or perhaps I should say "good hunting." You are, indeed, about to set out after elusive game. But I promise, the thrill of each new discovery will make the work more than worth the effort.

Recommended Reading

Certainly this is not a comprehensive reading list, but rather an attempt to point you toward some excellent reference and specialized "how to" books.

Finding a record is often of no use at all if you can't interpret the information or understand how to use it make your next research decision.

Self-education is a large part of genealogical work and I highly recommend that you build a reference library for yourself in addition to availing yourself of the many good online training tools available at sites like Ancestry.com and FamilySearch.org.

Aulicino, Emily D. *Genetic Genealogy: The Basics and Beyond*. AuthorHouse, 2013.

Board for Certification of Genealogists. *The BCG Genealogical Standards Manual*. Ancestry Publishing, 2000.

Burroughs, Tony. *Black Roots: A Beginner's Guide to Tracing the African American Family Tree*. Touchstone, 2001.

Carmack, Sharon DeBartolo. *A Genealogist's Guide to Discovering Your Female Ancestors: Special Strategies for Uncovering Hard-to-Find Information*. Betterway Books, 1998.

Carmack, Sharon DeBartolo. *Organizing Your Family History Search: Efficient & Effective Ways to Gather and Protect Your Genealogical Research*. Betterway Books, 1999.

Carmack, Sharon DeBartolo. *You Can Write Your Family History*. Genealogical Publishing Company, 2009.

Clifford, Karen. *Becoming an Accredited Genealogist: Plus 100 Tips to Ensure Your Success*. Ancestry Publishing, 1998.

Cole, Trafford R. *Italian Genealogical Records: How to Use Civil, Ecclesiastical & Other Records in Family History*. Ancestry Publishing, 1995.

Colletta, John Philip. *They Came in Ships: Finding Your Immigrant Ancestor's Arrival Record*. Ancestry.com, 2002.

Dolan, Allison. *The Family Tree Guidebook to Europe: Your Essential Guide to Trace Your Genealogy in Europe*. Family Tree Books, 2013.

Dollarhide, William. *Map Guide to American Migration Routes, 1735-1815*. Heritage Quest, 1997.

Durie, Bruce. *Scottish Genealogy*. The History Press, 2012.

Editors of Family Tree Magazine. *The Genealogist's Census Pocket Reference: Tips, Tricks & Fast Facts to Track Your Ancestors*. Family Tree Books, 2012.

Hansen, Kevan M. *Finding Your German Ancestors: A Beginner's Guide*. Ancestry.com, 2001.

Hendrickson, Nancy. *The Genealogist's U.S. History Pocket Reference: Quick Facts & Timelines of American History to Help Understand Your Ancestors*. Family Tree Books, 2013.

Hendrickson, Nancy. *The Unofficial Guide to Ancestry.com: How to Find Your Family History on the No. 1 Genealogy Website*. Family Tree Books, 2014.

Herber, Mark D. *Ancestral Trails: The Complete Guide to British Genealogy and Family History*. Genealogical Publishing Company, 1998

Levenick, Denise May. *How to Archive Family Keepsakes: Learn How to Preserve Family Photos, Memorabilia and Genealogy Records*. Family Tree Books, 2012.

Meyerink, Kory. *Printed Sources: A Guide to Published Genealogical Records*. Ancestry Publishing, 1998.

Mills, Elizabeth Shown. *Evidence Explained: Citing History Sources from Artifacts to Cyberspace, 2nd Edition*. Genealogical Publishing Company, Inc., 2009.

Morgan, George G. *Advanced Genealogy Research Techniques*. McGraw-Hill Osborne Media, 2013.

Nelson, Lynn. *Genealogists Guide to Discovering Your Italian Ancestors: How to Find and Record Your Unique Heritage*. F+W Media, 1997.

Powell, Kimberly. *The Everything Guide to Online Genealogy: Use the Web to Trace Your Roots, Share Your History, and Create a Family Tree*. Adams Media, 2011.

Quillen, W. Daniel. *Mastering Immigration & Naturalization Records*. Cold Spring Press, 2012.

Rising, Marsha Hoffman. *The Family Tree Problem Solver: Tried-and-True Tactics for Tracing Elusive Ancestors*. Family Tree Books, 2011.

Rose, Christine. *Courthouse Research for Family Historians: Your Guide to Genealogical Treasures*. CR Publications, 2001.

Rose, James M. *Black Genesis: A Resource Book for African-American Genealogy*. Genealogical Publishing Company, 2003.

Ryskamp, George R. *Finding Your Mexican Ancestors: A Beginner's Guide*. Ancestry.com, 2007.

Schaefer, Christina. *The Hidden Half of the Family: A Sourcebook for Women's Genealogy*. Genealogical Publishing Company, 1999.

Smolenyak, Megan and Ann Turner. *Trace Your Roots with DNA: Using Genetic Tests to Explore Your Family Tree*. Rodale Books, 2004.

Sperry, Kip. *Reading Early American Handwriting*. Genealogical Publishing Company, 2008.

Taylor, Maureen A. *Preserving Your Family Photographs*. Picture Perfect Press, 2010.

Taylor, Maureen A. *Family Photo Detective: Learn How to Find Genealogy Clues in Old Photos and Solve Family Photo Mysteries*. Family Tree Books, 2013.

Thorndale, William. *Map Guide to the U.S. Federal Censuses, 1790-1920*. Genealogical Publishing Company, 1995.

Wolper, Vickie Ellen. *Photograph Restoration and Enhancement Using Adobe Photoshop*. Mercury Learning and Information, 2013.

Woodtor, Dee Parmer. *Finding a Place Called Home: A Guide to African-American Genealogy and Historical Identity*. Random House Reference, 1999.

Conclusion

Thank you again for buying this book! I spent months writing it. As someone who has loved genealogy for years, friends told me to share my knowledge!

I hope this book helps you if you decide to start researching your family free and that you uncover many happy surprises.

If I've helped you - Please Can You Help Me....

Finally, if you enjoyed this book, please, please, please take the time to share your thoughts and post a review on whatever site you purchased it from. It will be greatly appreciated!

Don't Forget

I've got a great collection of genealogy videos that I'd like to share with you totally free.

Please just visit http://www.FreeGenealogyVideos.com – For your free videos

Index

Index

Free Genealogy Videos

Please Don't Forget...

I want to share with a fabulous collection of genealogy videos

Please just visit

www.FreeGenealogyVideos.com so we can email all the videos 100% free – just as an extra 'thank you' for purchasing this book.

The videos cover everything you need...

- Introduction
- Getting Started
- Evernote
- Roadblocks
- Research tricks
- Planning
- And lots more

Make sure you receive them all free at

www.FreeGenealogyVideos.com

14361416R00081

Printed in Great Britain
by Amazon.co.uk, Ltd.,
Marston Gate.